Junior Skill Builders

U.S. CONSTITUTION in 15 Minutes a Day

Related Titles

Algebra in 15 Minutes a Day
Basic Math in 15 Minutes a Day
Geometry in 15 Minutes a Day
Grammar in 15 Minutes a Day
Math Word Problems in 15 Minutes a Day
Reading in 15 Minutes a Day
Spelling in 15 Minutes a Day
Word Power in 15 Minutes a Day
Writing in 15 Minutes a Day

Junior Skill Builders

U.S. CONSTITUTION in 15 Minutes a Day

LearningExpress®

NEW YORK

Published in the United States by LearningExpress, LLC, New York.

Library of Congress Cataloging-in-Publication Data:
U.S. Constitution in 15 minutes a day. — 1st ed.
p. cm. — (Junior skill builders)
ISBN 978-1-57685-767-0
1. United States. Constitution—Juvenile literature. 2. United States. Constitution—Study and teaching (Middle school)—Juvenile literature. 3. United States—Politics and government—1775–1783—Juvenile literature. 4. United States—Politics and government—1775–1783—Study and teaching (Middle school) —Juvenile literature. 5. United States—Politics and government—1783–1789—Juvenile literature. 6. United States—Politics and government—1783–1789—Study and teaching (Middle school)—Juvenile literature. 7. Constitutional history—United States—Juvenile literature. 8. Constitutional history—United States—Study and teaching (Middle school) — Juvenile literature. I. LearningExpress (Organization) II. Title: United States Constitution in fifteen minutes a day.
E303.U557 2011
342.02071'2—dc22

2011000679

Printed in the United States of America

9 8 7 6 5 4 3 2 1

First Edition

ISBN 978-1-57685-767-0

For more information or to place an order, contact LearningExpress at:
2 Rector Street
26th Floor
New York, NY 10006

Or visit us at:
www.learnatest.com

CONTENTS

About the Contributor	vii
Introduction	1
Pretest	3
SECTION 1: HISTORY	7
Lesson 1: Before the Constitution	9
Lesson 2: The Founders	15
Lesson 3: Debating the Constitution	21
Lesson 4: Ratifying the Constitution	27
SECTION 2: ARTICLES	31
Lesson 5: The Preamble	33
Lesson 6: Article I	39
Lesson 7: Articles II–VII	47
SECTION 3: THE BILL OF RIGHTS	53
Lesson 8: The First Amendment	55
Lesson 9: The Second Amendment	61
Lesson 10: The Third and Fourth Amendments	67

Lesson 11: The Fifth Amendment 73

Lesson 12: The Sixth, Seventh, and Eighth Amendments 79

Lesson 13: The Ninth and Tenth Amendments 83

SECTION 4: THE ELEVENTH THROUGH TWENTY-THIRD AMENDMENTS 87

Lesson 14: The Eleventh and Twelfth Amendments 89

Lesson 15: The Thirteenth Amendment 95

Lesson 16: The Fourteenth Amendment 101

Lesson 17: The Fifteenth Amendment 107

Lesson 18: The Sixteenth and Seventeenth Amendments 111

Lesson 19: The Eighteenth and Twenty-First Amendments 115

Lesson 20: The Nineteenth Amendment 121

Lesson 21: The Twentieth, Twenty-Second, and Twenty-Third Amendments 125

Lesson 22: The Twenty-Fourth through Twenty-Seventh Amendments 131

Lesson 23: Pending and Unratified Amendments 135

Posttest 141

APPENDICES 145

Appendix A: Glossary 147

Appendix B: The Full Text of the Constitution, Bill of Rights, and the Amendments 151

Appendix C: List and Summary of Amendments 175

Appendix D: Timeline 177

about the contributor

AMANDA FRISS is a freelance writer, poet, and bookseller. She is the author of *Express Review Guides: Writing* and *Express Review Guides: Reading Comprehension*. Her work has also appeared in several literary journals. Currently, she resides in New York with her husband, Evan.

Junior Skill Builders

U.S. CONSTITUTION in 15 Minutes a Day

INTRODUCTION

HOW OFTEN DO you think about the Constitution in your daily life? Probably not very much. But just because many of us are not thinking about the Constitution when we raise our hand in class, watch election results come in, or gather together with friends, the fact is that the Constitution affects almost every part of our lives. Our entire government, the laws it makes, the judges who interpret them, and the rights and liberties we have are all determined by the Constitution.

Perhaps most remarkable of all, many of these rules we follow and rights we have were established hundreds of years ago by relatively few men, our Founders. When they wrote the Constitution, they decided what rights the people should have and the powers each branch of government should have. Who could vote? Who could be president? Can people carry guns? These were just some of the questions answered by the Constitution. But no matter how comprehensive the Founders were in setting up a government and securing the rights of the people, there were certain things that they could not have thought of. Luckily, they made sure that the Constitution was a flexible document, meaning that in future generations, when new problems or new beliefs arose, people could make changes. These changes, or amendments, have become an important part of the Constitution; providing some additional rights and altering some rules about how the government should operate.

Overall, the Constitution is the most important document in U.S. history. It is the Constitution that gave us a president instead of a king. It is the Constitution that gave us three branches of government: the president, senators and congresspeople, and Supreme Court judges.

It is the Constitution that ensures our right to free speech. It is the Constitution that officially ended slavery. It is the Constitution that gives women the right to vote. As you'll see throughout this book, many of the things that define our country, government, and society all come from the Constitution.

Before the lessons begin, you'll find a pretest, which you should complete before you move on. Don't worry—No one will be looking at your score. It's just there so that you can see how much you already know. At the end of the book there's a posttest, so you can see how much you've learned! Each lesson in between discusses some aspect of the creation of the Constitution or the Constitution itself, and it includes practice questions to help you remember what you learned. Each lesson should take you about 15 minutes to complete. After the posttest you'll find a glossary of terms, a list and summary of the amendments, a timeline of events, the full text of the Constitution, the Bill of Rights, and the amendments.

PRETEST

THE FOLLOWING TEST consists of multiple choice, matching, fill-in-the-blank, and true or false questions (30 in total) and is designed to measure how much you already know about the Constitution. Don't worry if you aren't sure of an answer. After all, you haven't even read the book yet! Once you have made your way through the lessons in this book and have completed the posttest at the end, you'll be able to see how much you've learned. The test should take you about 30 minutes and all the answers, along with lesson references, are at the end. Good luck!

Choose the best answer to the following questions.

1. When was the Constitution written?
 a. just before the Revolutionary War
 b. during the Civil War
 c. just after the Revolutionary War
 d. just after the Civil War

2. Where did the Constitutional Convention take place?
   a. Philadelphia
   b. Boston
   c. Washington, DC
   d. New York

3. Who are included in *the Founders*?
   a. the men who led the army during the Revolutionary War
   b. George Washington's father and grandfather
   c. the men who wrote the Constitution
   d. all of the above

4. Which of the following is NOT a power granted to Congress by the Constitution?
   a. to nominate Supreme Court judges
   b. to declare war
   c. to print money
   d. to establish post offices

5. What right is guaranteed to citizens of the United States by the First Amendment?
   a. right to bear arms
   b. right to vote
   c. right to a fair trial
   d. right to free speech

Match each term with its definition.

6. Bill of Rights	**a.** a person, not born in the United States, who legally becomes a citizen
7. involuntary servitude	**b.** period in history when alcohol was banned
8. Confederate	**c.** first 10 amendments
9. Prohibition	**d.** one of the houses of Congress
10. suffrage	**e.** the right to vote
11. naturalized citizen	**f.** a supporter of the states that had left the Union during the Civil War

12. Senate — g. one of the branches of government

13. judicial — h. forced labor

14. Preamble — i. a person who, during the Constitutional debate, felt the government had been given too much power

15. Anti-Federalist — j. introduction to the Constitution

Fill in the blank with the correct number.

16. The _____ Amendment bans cruel and unusual punishment.

17. The _____ Amendment repealed the Eighteenth Amendment.

18. The _____ Amendment grants citizens of Washington, DC the right to vote for president.

19. The _____ Amendment explains presidential election procedures.

20. The _____ Amendment provides for the direct election of Senators.

21. The _____ Amendment secures the right to bear arms.

22. The _____ Amendment establishes the voting age at 18 years old.

23. The _____ Amendment abolishes slavery.

24. The _____ Amendment limits the president to two terms in office.

25. The _____ Amendment secures the right for women to vote.

Decide whether each of the following statements is *true* or *false*.

26. Citizens have the right to refuse to let soldiers eat or sleep in their homes.

27. Citizens do not have the right to face their witnesses who are testifying against them at trial.

28. Citizens have the right not to be tried twice for the same crime.

29. Congress is not permitted to collect taxes from citizens' incomes.

30. Presidents are not allowed to serve nonconsecutive terms in office.

ANSWERS

1. **a** (Lesson 1)
2. **a** (Lesson 1)
3. **c** (Lesson 2)
4. **a** (Lesson 6)
5. **d** (Lesson 8)
6. **c** (Lesson 8)
7. **h** (Lesson 15)
8. **f** (Lesson 16)
9. **b** (Lesson 19)
10. **e** (Lesson 20)
11. **a** (Lesson 16)
12. **d** (Lesson 3)
13. **g** (Lesson 3)
14. **j** (Lesson 5)
15. **i** (Lesson 4)
16. **8** (Lesson 12)
17. **21** (Lesson 19)
18. **23** (Lesson 21)
19. **12** (Lesson 14)
20. **17** (Lesson 18)
21. **2** (Lesson 9)
22. **26** (Lesson 22)
23. **13** (Lesson 15)
24. **22** (Lesson 21)
25. **19** (Lesson 20)
26. **true.** The Third Amendment secures the right of citizens to refuse to allow soldiers to eat or sleep in their homes. (Lesson 10)
27. **false.** The Sixth Amendment secures the right of the accused to face witnesses at trial. (Lesson 12)
28. **true.** The Fifth Amendment secures the right to not stand trial for the same crime twice; also known as *double jeopardy*. (Lesson 11)
29. **false.** The Sixteenth Amendment allows Congress to collect income taxes. (Lesson 18)
30. **false.** The Twenty-second Amendment states that Presidents can serve only two terms, but they do not have to be consecutive. (Lesson 21)

SECTION 1

history

LESSON 1

before the constitution

Liberty, when it begins to take root, is a plant of rapid growth.
—GEORGE WASHINGTON

This lesson provides you with some background information about what was happening in the 13 American colonies leading up to the creation of the Constitution. There's also a tiny bio about the Founders just for a preview of Lesson 2.

WHEN YOU THINK of the Founders of the United States, you probably picture a bunch of old, white men with white wigs, sitting around debating the Constitution. In many ways, this is an accurate depiction, but in other ways it's not. Yes, they were all men, they were all white, and they did, in fact, sit around debating various systems of government, but they were not all old. Sometimes, it can be difficult to imagine that people living during the time of the American Revolution, way back in the 1700s, weren't all old—just as it's difficult to imagine that people you see in a black and white photograph were actually living in a world full of color. We think of a time long ago and tend to lump it all together as *history*. We don't stop to consider that perhaps the people living back then had more in common with us than we think. They may not have had e-mail and iPods and video games, but they had been kids just like you, who had gone to school while their parents worked (if they were lucky), and had tried to think of ways to improve the world around them.

Now, let's talk a little bit about what was happening at the time that made it necessary for these men to gather with the purpose of creating a new government.

Before the United States of America was its own country, it was a group of 13 colonies under British rule. This meant that the colonies were controlled by the British government. The British government at the time had a policy of *salutary neglect,* which basically meant that as long as everything was going well in the colonies, the British government would leave the colonies alone. This relationship lasted many years, until the British Empire, desperate for money, began to tax the colonies.

DEFINITION If something is **salutary,** it produces a beneficial result. So, **salutary neglect** is neglect that produces a beneficial result. The British government adopted this policy with the belief that their colonies, left alone, would flourish.

Now, imagine you're a colonist, and for years the British government has left you alone across the Atlantic Ocean to do as you please. You've been creating businesses, raising a family, growing food on farms, and, if you were a white male landowner, participating in your local government. You've created a life for yourself and your family. Now, all of a sudden the British government needs money, so you have to give it to them. As you might imagine, this made people upset. Not only was the British government demanding money, but the colonists were not even represented in the British Parliament (law-making body), so they didn't have any say in what the money was used for. This *taxation without representation* created a growing resistance. In September 1774, the First Continental Congress met in Philadelphia. The purpose of the meeting was for representatives of the colonies to get together and make sure they were united in their resistance to the British government's taxation without representation.

FUN FACT One of the new taxes placed on the colonists by the British, called the *Stamp Act,* required all printed goods to have a stamp on them. This involved everything from playing cards to legal documents. Imagine you are a newspaper publisher living in Boston in 1765. How do you think you would feel about the Stamp Act?

The Revolutionary War began in 1775, and two years later the Second Continental Congress established a basic system that would allow the colonies to make decisions as a unified group. They didn't set up a system of government; instead, they created the **Articles of Confederation**. The document was drafted in 1777 and ratified in 1781. (See the timeline on page 178.)

DEFINITION Ratify to approve formally

The colonies had declared independence from British rule in 1776, and the Articles of Confederation served as a way for the colonies to co-exist without an overriding government. Under the Articles of Confederation, each colony would have one vote, and all major decisions required 9 out of the 13 colonies to approve them. In order to make amendments (changes) to the Articles, there had to be unanimous (total) consent among the colonies. Since a unanimous vote (13 to 0) was so difficult to get, there were no amendments made to the Articles during the seven years they were in effect.

By May 1787, there had been a lot of talk among various political leaders in the colonies about how the Articles of Confederation needed strengthening. Many thought that there needed to be a central government that had the power to organize and help bring about functions for the country as a whole. Representatives met again in Philadelphia to *amend* (change) the Articles. During this meeting, called the Constitutional Convention, the representatives decided that amending the Articles of Confederation wouldn't work. They needed to scrap them and start over with a brand new constitution.

PRACTICE 1

1. Which one describes *salutary neglect*?
  a. The colonists had a habit of not feeding their children.
  b. The British government had left the colonists alone as long as everything was going well.
  c. The British government neglected to tell the colonists that they would be taxed.
  d. The colonists didn't know what was going on in Britain.

2. Why were colonists upset about the new taxes started by the British government?
  a. They were too complicated.
  b. They thought that different items should be taxed.
  c. They resented the British government's involvement in their affairs without their having representation in the British government.
  d. They were lazy and didn't want to fill out the tax forms.

3. What was the purpose of the First Continental Congress?
a. to declare war on the British
b. to create a Constitution for the United States
c. to decide which colonies would send representatives to the British Parliament
d. to coordinate tax resistance efforts

4. According to the rules of the Articles of Confederation, how many colonies needed to approve an amendment?
a. 0
b. 11
c. 13
d. 10

5. What was the original purpose of the Constitutional Convention?
a. to elect a leader of the Continental army
b. to revise the Articles of Confederation
c. to create a Constitution
d. to honor those who had died in the war

For questions **6** through **10**, identify whether each statement is either *true* or *false*.

6. There were many amendments to the Articles of Confederation.

7. Colonists were thrilled about the new taxes imposed by the British government.

8. The Articles of Confederation did not create a system of government for the colonies.

9. The Founders were all old.

10. Many people in 1787 thought the Articles of Confederation needed strengthening.

ANSWERS

1. **b.** While it is true that the British government probably neglected to inform the colonists of the upcoming taxes, the term salutary neglect refers to the policy of the British government to leave the colonists alone as long as everything was going well.
2. **c.** After years of being left to their own business, the colonists were upset that the British were suddenly meddling in their affairs.
3. **d.** Representatives from the colonies wanted to make sure they were all on the same page regarding tax resistance.
4. **c.** Under the terms of the Articles of Confederation, all 13 colonies needed to approve any major decision.
5. **b.** Although the colonists ended up discarding the Articles of Confederation and starting over, the original purpose of the Constitutional Convention was to amend the existing Articles.
6. **false.** Since there needed to be a unanimous vote in order to amend the Articles of Confederation, there were never any amendments made.
7. **false.** Colonists were certainly not thrilled.
8. **true.** While the Constitution later established a system of government for the United States, the Articles of Confederation did not.
9. **false.** Not all the Founders were old. In fact, most were relatively young.
10. **true.** This was the reason that the Constitutional Convention met in Philadelphia in 1787. Many people believed that the Articles of Confederation was not sufficient in its present form as a document that created a strong national government.

And now we're back to where we started in this lesson, a bunch of men sitting around trying to come up with a new form of government. As you might imagine, our Founders all had strong opinions about what the system of government should look like and they debated the issues passionately.

Let's take a look at who these Founders, the key players in the constitutional debate, were.

LESSON 2

the founders

Associate with men of good quality if you esteem your own reputation; for it is better to be alone than in bad company.
—GEORGE WASHINGTON

This lesson gives you a little glimpse into the lives of five men who were among the most important Founders of our country. You'll learn what they were up to in the years leading up to the Constitutional Convention and the campaign that followed to ratify the Constitution.

NOW THAT YOU know all about what was going on in America before it actually became a country, let's go back to that picture in our minds of all the old men, our Founders. At the Constitutional Convention in 1787, there were 55 men in attendance. The average age was just 44 years old, which may seem old to you, but they certainly weren't the old men whom we often think of when we picture those who created our Constitution. They were, however, all white and nearly all well-educated. More than half the delegates had college degrees, which was pretty unusual, since less than one-tenth of one percent of the population at the time had attended college. Also, 22 of the 55 delegates had served in the Continental army during the Revolution, so these men weren't just intellectuals; many had been soldiers, too.

You will read about five of these men who were important to the creation of our Constitution. You will most likely recognize their names; some of them even appear on U.S. money. They are the men we credit with creating our current system of government, the one established by the Constitution. Not only were they the brains behind the operation, but they had the necessary skills to convince the other delegates to accept their ideas about government.

GEORGE WASHINGTON

George Washington was not just the first President of the United States. His career in the military during the Revolutionary War had made him a celebrity throughout the colonies before he ascended to the presidency. His heroism, intelligence, and gentlemanly manner made him a much admired statesman.

Born in 1732 to a wealthy Virginia family, George Washington became a lieutenant colonel in the military when he was only 22 years old. Then, in the years leading up to the Revolutionary War, Washington served in Virginia's colonial government. By the time the Constitutional Convention rolled around in 1787, he had gained the respect of the colonists. Many colonies sent delegates to the convention only because they knew that George Washington would be there. His name alone lent legitimacy to the proceedings. All debates need a moderator, and that was George Washington's role. He pretty much ran the show at the convention, keeping everyone in line and the discussion moving toward progress.

After the convention had ended, Washington would have preferred to go home to Mount Vernon, Virginia, with his wife Martha and live a quiet life. However, he was elected to be our first president and took office in 1789 at the age of 57. The fact that Washington wasn't particularly interested in such a powerful position made him all the more popular in the eyes of the public.

THOMAS JEFFERSON

Although Thomas Jefferson is indeed considered one of our country's Founders, he did not actually attend the Convention of 1787. He was serving as minister to France at the time, so he was living overseas.

Born in 1743 in Virginia, Jefferson attended the College of William and Mary, studied law, and in 1772 got married and settled into his home, Monticello, on a mountaintop surrounded by 5,000 acres of land that he had inherited from his father. Jefferson was a wonderful writer but awkward as a public speaker, so he did most of his speaking with a pen, rather than with his voice. Like George Washington, he was a member of Virginia's colonial government and the Continental Congress. In 1776 when he was only 33 years old, Thomas Jefferson drafted the Declaration of Independence.

Although Jefferson wasn't actually present at the Constitutional Convention of 1787, many of his ideas were. Unlike Founder Alexander Hamilton, who believed in a strong national government, Jefferson believed in strong state governments and also in a separation between church and state. He kept tabs on what was going on by way of letters to and from France. He would later serve as Secretary of State under George Washington. In 1801, he became the third president of the United States.

BENJAMIN FRANKLIN

Born in 1706, Benjamin Franklin was the oldest delegate at the Constitutional Convention. He was 81 years old and had a whole lifetime of experience and wisdom to share at the debate.

Franklin spent his early years as an apprentice in the printing trade and went on to make printing his career. But he wasn't just a printer; he was an inventor, a writer, a scientist, and even a swimmer. (He even invented a pair of swimming fins.) He was curious about the world around him, loved to read, and always enjoyed learning and discovering new things. In 1748, he retired from printing and focused on his other interests. Eighteen years later, at the age of 60, Franklin was elected a member of the prestigious Royal Society.

FUN FACT Benjamin Franklin is in the International Swimming Hall of Fame.

Like Jefferson, Benjamin Franklin was a diplomatic representative to France. But he was back in Philadelphia in 1787 for the Constitutional Convention, where he urged the delegates to sign the final document. He was also a big believer in the abolition of slavery, and at the age of 81, he became the president of The Society for Promoting the Abolition of Slavery and the Relief of Negroes Unlawfully Held in Bondage. Franklin died in 1790, not long after the Constitution was ratified. He was 84 years old.

JAMES MADISON

Only thirty-six years old in 1787, James Madison was one of the youngest delegates at the Constitutional Convention, and one of the most outspoken. He participated frequently in the lively debates, and his ideas were probably the most influential.

Madison was raised in Virginia and attended Princeton University, where he became well versed in the subjects of history and government. He later read law on his own. In 1776, he helped write Virginia's state constitution and then served in both the Continental Congress and the Virginia General Assembly. Madison believed in a strong central government and in states' rights. In order to convince New Yorkers to ratify the Constitution, he co-wrote the ***Federalist Papers*** with Alexander Hamilton and John Jay. Although originally published in New York newspapers, The *Federalist Papers* were circulated among the colonies during the year between the creation of the Constitution and its ratification. They helped to convince people that ratification was necessary.

James Madison served as Thomas Jefferson's secretary of state and he would become our country's fourth president in 1809.

FUN FACT Many historians believe that James Madison was a hypochondriac. (*Hypochondria* is a disorder that causes a person to believe they have imaginary physical ailments.)

ALEXANDER HAMILTON

Alexander Hamilton has a rags-to-riches story. He had been born on the island of Nevis in the Caribbean in 1757 and spent his youth as a humble clerk surrounded by the wealth from sugar plantations. His father left when he was eight and his mother died when he was 11. Fortunately for Hamilton, at the age of 16, someone sponsored him to travel to New York to attend King's College (which is now Columbia University). The opportunity changed his life. He became a lawyer, founded New York's first bank, and joined the military in 1775.

At the Constitutional Convention, Hamilton argued for a strong central government, even admitting that he would prefer a monarchy. He later co-authored the *Federalist Papers* with James Madison and John Jay. In 1789, Hamilton was appointed secretary of the treasury in George Washington's administration, where he helped establish a more modern financial system. In

1804, Hamilton died a dramatic death at the age of forty-seven when he was killed by Vice President Aaron Burr in a duel.

ACTIVITY If you could invite one of these Founders over for dinner, which one would you choose and why?

PRACTICE 1

For questions **1–5** match the Founder with his identity.

1. Ben Franklin	**a.** was not born in the United States
2. James Madison	**b.** printer by day, scientist by night
3. Alexander Hamilton	**c.** the fourth president
4. Thomas Jefferson	**d.** was a heroic general in the army
5. George Washington	**e.** was not present at the Convention

Answer either *true* or *false* for questions **6–10**.

6. Thomas Jefferson was in favor of a strong central government.
7. Alexander Hamilton disagreed with what was written in the *Federalist Papers*.
8. George Washington moderated the debates at the Constitutional Convention.
9. James Madison was a co-author of the *Federalist Papers*.
10. Benjamin Franklin was the youngest delegate at the convention.

ANSWERS

1. b. Franklin was not just a printer. He was also a scientist.
2. c. Madison was the fourth president of the United States.
3. a. Hamilton was born on the Caribbean island of Nevis.
4. e. Jefferson was in France during the Constitutional Convention.
5. d. Washington was a national hero after his career in the army.

6. false. Jefferson was wary of a strong federal government. He felt that the strongest powers should be reserved for the states.

7. false. Hamilton certainly agreed with most of what was written in the *Federalist Papers*. He had been one of the authors.

8. true. As the admired general and gentleman, Washington served as a moderator of the debates at the Constitutional Convention.

9. true. Madison co-wrote the *Federalist Papers*.

10. false. Franklin was actually the oldest delegate at the Constitutional Convention.

LESSON 3

debating the constitution

An association of men who will not quarrel with one another is a thing which has never yet existed, from the greatest confederacy of nations down to a town meeting or vestry.

—THOMAS JEFFERSON

This lesson discusses the major topics for debate at the Constitutional Convention of 1787 and explains the thinking behind some of the most influential philosophies introduced there.

IMAGINE THE PEOPLE in charge of your school decided to do away with the current rules and regulations to which you and your classmates have become accustomed. They ask for representatives from each class to help create a new kind of school. Imagine that you will be one of these representatives. Think about all the decisions that you and your fellow delegates will have to make. You will have to come to a consensus on everything: how much time should be spent in classes, between them, at lunch, and what the system will be for hiring teachers. I'm sure you can imagine the debates that would arise with all the different personalities and philosophies together in one room. This is basically what happened at the Constitutional Convention. Our Founders debated all the details of what our new government would be.

PRACTICE 1

Write a very brief answer to the following questions.

1. Considering what you learned in Lesson 1, name one thing you think the delegates might have been concerned about with regard to the new government they were creating.

2. List three topics that you would have liked to discuss if you had been present at the debate.

ANSWERS

The following are some possible answers to the questions.

1. Considering their history with Britain, the delegates might have been concerned with taxes or with making sure that their own people would have the power in the new government.

2. Some possible topics that would relate to the formation of a new government are: the presidential election process, involvement of ordinary people in the government, and safeguards for people's rights.

As we discussed earlier, when our Founders got together in that room in Philadelphia in May 1787, their assigned task was to amend the existing Articles of Confederation. But when they all started talking, the majority decided that amending the Articles wouldn't be good enough. They needed to start over with a blank slate.

This is when the debate really started. Now they weren't just tweaking an existing document; they were creating a whole new system of government. And, as you might imagine, there were many varying opinions about how this new system of government should operate.

There were four points, however, on which the delegates agreed right off the bat.

1. The new constitution would create a legislative, an executive, and a judicial branch.

2. The new government would be allowed to raise money without the consent of the states.

3. States would not be permitted to violate the property rights of their citizens.

4. The new government must represent the people.

AN ELITE GOVERNMENT

Though the delegates agreed on these four points, the debate dragged on. There were so many other ideas and values to consider when they were creating a government from scratch. One value that was evident during the course of the discussion was that of **elitism**.

The 55 men gathered in Philadelphia that spring were all fairly financially well-off according to the standards of the time and, as discussed earlier, many had advanced degrees. These people who founded our country were certainly an elite group, and they had in mind that the government should be made up of men like themselves. This influenced the rules that they established.

THE VIRGINIA PLAN VERSUS THE NEW JERSEY PLAN

Edmund Randolph proposed a plan, which became known as **The Virginia Plan**, since he was representing Virginia. This plan, drafted by the Virginia delegates under the leadership of James Madison, called for a *bicameral* (two-house) legislature (law-making body). Within each house, states would be awarded a number of representatives based on their population. Understandably, delegates from the smaller states didn't like this idea, because it would give them less representation in the government. A delegate from New Jersey proposed a different plan (named, of course, **The New Jersey Plan**), which suggested a unicameral (single-house) legislature in which each state received one vote.

Eventually they came to a great compromise. There would be two houses of government, the **Senate** and the **House of Representatives**. The Senate would have two representatives from each state, regardless of population. The number of representatives from a particular state in the House of Representatives would be determined according to the population of that state.

FUN FACTS Maybe you're wondering how we know what went on at the Convention. Well, it was indeed a closed-room meeting. (Literally, they kept the windows closed for secrecy, which also meant that the room got very hot in the middle of the Philadelphia summer.) No one except the delegates was allowed in the room. Luckily for us, James Madison felt the importance of the meeting and took very careful notes. Several other delegates kept less extensive notes as well.

SLAVERY

Slavery was a hot topic at the Constitutional debate. In fact, some states (like South Carolina) showed up defending slavery among their goals. They were afraid that the new government would abolish a system on which they depended both economically and socially. Some of the compromises that were made on the issue are described later in this book.

FEDERALISM

One main point of disagreement among the delegates was centered on the balance of power between the state and central governments. Until this time, each state possessed a lot of power, since there had been no overriding central government. Much of the debate rested on this issue. How much power should be given to the *federal* (central) government and how much should remain with the states? Not only did people have different ideas about the balance of power, but they had different ideas of how to achieve that balance.

The term **federalism** refers to the relationship between state and central authority. Since the delegates' goal was to create a central government that would govern alongside the existing state governments, they weren't quite sure where the greater power should be—with the states or with the central government. This was an important issue to the men congregated at the Convention because of the way the British government had treated them in the past. They were afraid that state and central governments would essentially be competing with each other for power.

James Madison, who as we learned in the previous lesson, participated actively in the debate, suggested that at the core the power should rest with the people. He pointed out that the delegates needed to create a government that gave some specific powers to the central government and left the rest to the states, which previously had had *all* the power. Both levels of government would be bound by the Constitution. The people could give powers this way, because the people were *sovereign*.

DEFINITION **Sovereignty** having supreme power.

SEPARATION OF POWERS

Keep in mind that up until this time, there was no effective central government in existence. Part of the reason the colonies had fought the war with Britain was to gain independence from what they felt was a tyrannical system. That is why they had been so hesitant to grant further powers to the Confederation congress. The delegates wanted to make sure that whatever government they created wouldn't become so powerful that the people of the country no longer had any control. This is where **federalism** and the **separation of powers** came in.

The chief check on the central government would be the states, which would retain most of the powers of government. The distribution of power between the central and the state governments, *federalism*, established this division of powers.

It was also important to the delegates to set up a situation where each of the three branches of the central government checked and balanced the other two branches. These **checks and balances** were supposed to insure that the central government would not become too oppressive.

FUN FACT The word *constitution* in eighteenth-century Britain did not refer to an actual document. It meant just the current system of British government and how it operated. Americans wanted an actual document. If their leaders were behaving badly, they could refer back to the written words as proof of how the system should work.

As you can see, the men at the Constitutional Convention had a lot of heavy philosophical ideas to debate. They entered into the task of creating a national government with a bit of uncertain agitation. They knew what they didn't want: (1) They didn't want the rights of the people to be overshadowed by the central government; (2) they didn't want any one branch of the government to be too powerful; and (3) they didn't want just any person off the street to be a leader. So they debated. They tossed around ideas for four months until they came up with what was essentially a brief outline of their new government. It was the Constitution.

Their job wasn't over yet, though. They might've come up with a whole new government, but now they had to convince the voters in the rest of the country that the Constitution was a good idea.

PRACTICE 2

Fill in the blanks for questions **1–5** with a word or phrase from the following list.

power
checks and balances
federalism
New Jersey
Virginia

1. The ______________ Plan proposed a unicameral (one-house) legislature.

2. ______________ is the relationship between the state and national governments.

3. In order to make sure that no one branch of government would overpower another, the delegates felt there should be ______________.

4. The ______________ Plan proposed a bicameral (two-house) legislature.

5. Most of the debate centered on ideas about where ____________ should lie.

ANSWERS

1. New Jersey
2. federalism
3. checks and balances
4. Virginia
5. power

LESSON 4

ratifying the constitution

A pen is certainly an excellent instrument to fix a man's attention and to inflame his ambition.
—JOHN ADAMS

This lesson explains what happened between the time the Constitution was created and when it was ratified (approved). It explains the two sides of the argument that took place regarding whether the Constitution provided enough protection for the rights and liberties of the country's citizens.

THE LAST SESSION of the Constitutional Convention was September 17, 1787. Having painstakingly created a new system of government for their brand new country, the delegates went home to their respective states. There was one final step in the process, however: The Constitution needed to be *ratified* (approved).

Nine of the 13 states needed to approve the Constitution for it to take effect. So, each state had an election to decide who from their state would act as their representatives at their state's ratifying convention. During this period of time—after the Constitutional Convention, before the ratifying convention, and while states were having their elections (see timeline on page 178)—many of the same debates that had once been confined to a single room in Philadelphia were happening across the country.

Some people were happy with the Constitution just as it was, with a large, strong national government that contained a self-regulating system of checks and balances. These people were called **Federalists**. Others felt that the Constitution gave the national government too much power and that the rights of the people would not be protected. These people were called **Anti-Federalists**. Let's take a closer look at these two sides of the debate.

FEDERALISTS

Alexander Hamilton, James Madison, and John Jay were among the Federalist spokesmen in support of ratifying the Constitution. Together they secretly authored what became known as the *Federalist Papers*. The series of 85 essays, published in various newspapers and magazines, appeared under the ghost name, Publius. Hamilton wrote 50 of the essays, Madison wrote 30, and Jay wrote 5. These essays, published all together in a book in 1788, are a collection of some of the most important political thought in our nation's history. They weren't just about the technical aspects of a government; they were about the ideas behind it all. Specifically, they were very much interested in finding an answer to the question of how the government can serve to protect the rights of the people. (*Remember:* They felt the British had trampled on their rights.)

Hamilton and the other Federalists believed that the Constitution did not endanger the liberties of the people, but rather protected them. One argument Madison made in support of this point was that since the United States was so large and diverse, it was impossible for any one school of thought to gain enough power to oppress anybody.

ANTI-FEDERALISTS

The Anti-Federalists believed that power given to the government would end up oppressing people. They felt that they were sticking up for the common people. They were worried that the rich and powerful people in the government would end up trampling on the rights of everyday citizens. Lacking leaders like Hamilton and Madison, the Anti-Federalist movement didn't get its message out to as many people. Of the 92 newspapers and magazines that existed at the time, only 12 published articles in support of the Anti-Federalist cause.

As it was, the Constitution was not good enough for the Anti-Federalists. They wanted a bill of rights, to be sure that certain liberties like freedom of speech and trial by jury were protected. Madison thought that federalism, the delegation of some powers to the federal government and the reservation of the rest of the powers to the states, along with the checks and balances among the branches of the federal government, would protect the rights of the people. Still, he eventually joined other Federalists in pledging that the first Congress to meet after ratification would recommend a bill of rights to the states for their ratification. This promise swayed some, but by no means all, Anti-Federalists toward ratification.

ACTIVITY If you had been around at the time, would you have been a Federalist or an Anti-Federalist? Why?

By the middle of 1788, nine states had ratified the new Constitution, making it the new law of the land. In the end, only two of the 13 states voted against ratification—North Carolina and Rhode Island. Of course, those two eventually ratified as well, or else they would not be part of the United States today.

PRACTICE 1

For questions **1–5** decide whether each idea is *Federalist* or *Anti-Federalist*.

1. large government protects liberties ____________________

2. bill of rights ____________________

3. diversity of interests protects from oppression ____________________

4. checks and balances are enough to protect liberties ____________________

5. smaller government is better ____________________

For questions **6–10** decide whether each statement is *true* or *false*.

6. James Madison felt that the Constitution needed a bill of rights.

7. The *Federalist Papers* were published in only 12 newspapers and magazines across the country.

8. Nine out of 13 states needed to ratify the Constitution in order for it to take effect.

9. The only states that at first voted not to ratify the Constitution were Rhode Island and North Carolina.

10. When the Constitution was ratified it contained a Bill of Rights.

ANSWERS

1. **Federalist.** The Federalists believed that the sheer size of the government protected the rights of the people.
2. **Anti-Federalist.** The Anti-Federalists believed that the Constitution needed to have a bill of rights.
3. **Federalist.** Madison, a Federalist, made the argument that the large diversity of opinions protects any one group from becoming too powerful.
4. **Federalist.** The Federalists believed that the division of powers between the federal government and the states, the supreme nature of the federal government, the voting rights nature of the government, and the checks and balances within the federal government were enough to protect people's liberties.
5. **Anti-Federalist.** Anti-Federalists believed that a large government would gain too much power over the people and, therefore, a smaller government was better.
6. **false.** James Madison did not think the Constitution needed a Bill of Rights. He believed the federal government would protect people's rights.
7. **false.** *The Federalist Papers* were published in many more than 12 publications. Articles supporting Anti-Federalist ideas were published in only 12 publications nationwide.
8. **true.** Only nine of the 13 states needed to ratify the Constitution for it to take effect.
9. **true.** Rhode Island and North Carolina were the only states that voted against ratification.
10. **false.** When the Constitution was ratified it did not contain a Bill of Rights. In order to gain Anti-Federalist support, Federalists—including James Madison—promised that a Bill of Rights would be proposed to the states for their ratification by the first Congress under the new Constitution.

SECTION 2

articles

LESSON 5

the preamble

The Constitution of the United States was made not merely for the generation that then existed, but for posterity, unlimited, undefined, endless, perpetual posterity.

—Henry Clay

This lesson introduces you to the Preamble of the Constitution. It explains what a Preamble is and breaks down its meaning, phrase by phrase. (For the complete text of the Constitution, refer to Appendix B at the end of this book.)

YOU'RE PROBABLY already a little familiar with the Preamble of the Constitution, since it is so often quoted. But maybe you're wondering what exactly *is* a preamble? Well, a standard dictionary definition of *preamble* is "an introductory statement; especially the introductory part of a constitution or statute that usually states the reasons for and intent of the law." So, the Preamble to the Constitution of the United States is essentially just an introduction to the Constitution itself. It gives us some basic information, like who is creating the document and for what reasons. First, we'll take a look at the Preamble as a whole and then we'll break it down into smaller pieces to help you understand what it means.

> *We the people of the United States, in order to form a more perfect Union, establish Justice, insure domestic Tranquility, provide for the common defense, promote the general Welfare, and secure the Blessings of Liberty to ourselves and our Posterity, do ordain and establish this Constitution for the United States of America.*

The first phrase in the Preamble tells us who is creating the Constitution.

We the people of the United States . . .

Although, as you learned in the previous lessons, the Constitution was in fact written by a select group of people, it was to be ratified by popular conventions in all the states. Thus, it was to be carried out by the people. Having seen how the absence of popular ratification weakened the Confederation government in conflicts with the state governments, the writers wanted to make sure that the Constitution came from "the people."

FUN FACT Originally, this section of the Preamble was written as "We the people of the states of New Hampshire, Massachusetts, New York, and so on," but the delegates changed it to "United States" in case some state or states decided not to ratify.

The next part of the Preamble contains a list of reasons why the Constitution is being written and what it is intended to accomplish. Here they are in list form.

In order to form a more perfect Union
Establish Justice
Insure domestic Tranquility
Provide for the common defense
Promote the general Welfare
Secure the Blessings of Liberty to ourselves and our Posterity

What do you notice about the first item on the list? You might have noticed that the Founders chose to include the word "more," instead of just "to form a Union" or even "to form a perfect Union." Their use of the word *more* implies that they felt the current union was satisfactory. They just wanted to make it better. They wanted to make it "more perfect." Also, the Constitution was originally intended to be a revision of the Articles of Confederation, which had already established a kind of union. The Constitution would make that union more perfect.

The second item on the list is "to establish Justice." This is a reference to the aspects of government laid out in the Constitution that deal both directly and indirectly with the justice system of the United States. It is also a reference to justice in general, or fairness, not only in the court system, but in social, political, and economic parts of society.

"Insure domestic Tranquility" is the third item on the list. As you can see, this, like many of the other statements in the Preamble, has a pretty broad meaning and could be interpreted in many ways. "Domestic" means having to do with the home and "tranquil" means calm. So, one of the purposes of the Constitution is to empower the United States government to intervene in case of war among states or insurrection within a state—both of which had happened during the Confederation period.

The fourth item on the list is also fairly self-explanatory. "To provide for the common defense" means to set up a system whereby the citizens of the United States will be protected by their government. Also, a stronger, more centralized government could create a military that hadn't existed under the Articles of Confederation.

According to the Preamble, another purpose of the Constitution is to "promote the general Welfare" of the people. This means that the Constitution is meant to create a situation that is generally beneficial to everyone. Again, you might notice that this is a general statement. There are no specifics in the Preamble about how exactly the Constitution will be beneficial, but it is just an introduction. All of the specifics are spelled out later.

The last item on the list was perhaps the reason that the whole process had begun in the first place. As you'll recall from previous lessons, our Founders were newly independent of the reign of the British government and because of this, the writers felt it was important to "secure the Blessings of Liberty" not only for themselves, but also for their "posterity," or future generations.

ACTIVITY Did you notice that some words in the Preamble are capitalized when normally they wouldn't be? These are what you might call *key* words, or words that the Founders wanted to emphasize. Go through the Preamble and read only the capitalized words. You'll get a good sense of what the Constitution is all about.

Now, having read the Preamble, you should know a little bit about what the Constitution was intended to accomplish. As you go through the lessons that follow, you'll see specific examples of ways the Founders (and following law makers) sought to create the kind of society that is outlined in the Preamble.

Practice 1

1. Write the letters of the following phrases in order, to form the Preamble of the Constitution.

a. and secure the Blessings of Liberty to ourselves and our Posterity
b. in order to form a more perfect Union
c. do ordain and establish this Constitution for the United States of America
d. We the people of the United States
e. establish Justice
f. promote the general Welfare
g. provide for the common defense
h. insure domestic Tranquility

2. What is a preamble?

a. conclusion
b. an introduction
c. a rant
d. a law

3. Why is the word *more* included in the phrase "a more perfect union"?

a. The Founders thought it sounded better.
b. The Preamble was too short without it.
c. There was already a union in place that was to be made better by the Constitution.
d. It was Benjamin Franklin's favorite word.

4. *Domestic tranquility* most closely means

a. peace at home
b. peace abroad
c. war at home
d. war abroad

For questions **5** through **10**, decide whether each statement is *true* or *false*.

5. One of the reasons the Constitution was created was to provide for the common defense.

6. The Preamble explains how the President will be elected.

7. The Preamble has nothing to do with the rest of the Constitution.

8. The Founders were only creating the Constitution for themselves, leaving future generations in charge of securing their own liberty.

9. The Preamble is one long sentence.

10. The term *posterity* refers to future generations.

11. Using the following list of words, fill in the blanks of the Preamble.

Tranquility
Defense
Union
Justice
Liberty

We the people of the United States, in order to form a more perfect ________, establish ________, insure domestic __________, provide for the common ____________, promote the general Welfare, and secure the Blessings of __________ to ourselves and our Posterity, do ordain and establish this Constitution for the United States of America.

ANSWERS

1. **d, b, e, h, g, f, a, c**
2. **b.** The Preamble is an introduction to the Constitution.
3. **c.** There was already a union that was established by the Articles of Confederation, but the Founders wanted to improve on that union.
4. **a.** *Domestic* means related to the home and *tranquility* means peace.
5. **true**
6. **false.** Nowhere in the Preamble does it say anything about how the president is elected.
7. **false.** The Preamble has a lot to do with the rest of the Constitution. It introduces and outlines the reasons the Constitution is being written.
8. **false.** The Preamble clearly states that the Constitution intends to "secure the Blessings of Liberty to ourselves and our Posterity."
9. **true**

10. true

11. We the people of the United States, in order to form a more perfect *Union*, establish *Justice*, insure domestic *Tranquility*, provide for the common *Defense*, promote the general Welfare, and secure the Blessings of *Liberty* to ourselves and our Posterity, do ordain and establish this Constitution for the United States of America.

LESSON 6

article i

To live under the American Constitution is the greatest political privilege that was ever accorded the human race.

—CALVIN COOLIDGE

This lesson discusses the 10 sections that make up Article I of the U.S. Constitution. You will learn from this part of the Constitution some of the basic structures of the government and some of the rules set in place by the Founders having to do with the Senate and the House of Representatives. You will also learn how a bill becomes a law.

IN THE PREVIOUS lesson you learned that the Preamble of the Constitution is an introduction. It gives the reader an idea of the reasons why the document has been created. Following the Preamble are the Articles. These Articles are the meat of the Constitution. They are where the ideas in the Preamble are expanded upon and where details about how our government will operate are laid out. What follows in the next two lessons is what was originally written, but many of the rules and regulations have been changed and amended since then.

The Constitution is composed of seven articles, and some of the articles are further divided into sections. In this lesson we start by focusing on Article I, which is divided into 10 sections.

Section 1

Section 1 is very short and says the following:

> *All legislative Powers herein granted shall be vested in a Congress of the United States, which shall consist of a Senate and a House of Representatives.*

So, Section 1 of Article I of the Constitution states that there will be a Congress of the United States that is made up of two houses, a Senate and a House of Representatives.

Section 2

Section 2 explains a little more about how the House of Representatives will work. Members of the House will be elected every two years, must be at least 25 years old, and have been citizens of the United States for at least seven years. Also, in order to be elected to represent a state in the House of Representatives, a person must be a resident of that state.

That takes care of who will be in the House of Representatives, but there is still the question of representation. Section 2 explains that the number of members representing each state will be based on the population of that state.

FUN FACT In 2010 the United States completed a Census, which counts the number of people residing in each state. Section 2 of Article I of the Constitution declares that a Census should be taken every ten years in order to keep the population count accurate, since each state's representation in the House is based on population.

This section of the Constitution also details who will be counted, for political purposes, as a person residing in any given state. You'd think this would be easy. A person is a person. But keep in mind that, at the time, some states allowed only white men to vote. They were the only people involved in the political process in those states. So there was a debate about what people would count as *people* for the purposes of deciding how many representatives a state would have. The Founders compromised by adding the clause "Three-fifths of all other Persons." In this instance *other Persons* refers to slaves. When this part of the Constitution was being debated, the states in the South (where most of the slaves were) wanted slaves to be counted just like everyone else, as whole people. This would have upped their population numbers, giving them more representatives in the government. States in the North didn't want slaves to count toward the population total, since they didn't have any political power anyway. So, having slaves count as three-fifths of a person was a compromise.

FUN FACT Did you notice how the Founders used the phrase *other Persons* instead of the word *slaves*? Why do you think they did this?

Section 3

Section 3 talks about the Senate and explains that each state will get two senators, each serving for a six-year term. Senators must be at least 30 years old, have been citizens of the United States for at least nine years, and be resident of the states they represent. The vice president of the country is the president of the Senate and, while each senator gets one vote, the President of the Senate gets to vote only if there's a tie. An interesting thing to note about this section of Article I is that the Founders stated that each senator would be chosen by the legislature of the state, which is not how the system works today. Today, as you might know, citizens elect their senators. The men who created the Constitution wanted to give the state governments the task of choosing senators in order to enable them to guard against congressional attempts to grab at the states' reserved powers. They were afraid that Congress would want to take the states' powers for itself.

FUN FACT You might have noticed the differences between the qualifications needed to become a member of the House of Representatives and the qualifications needed to become a member of the Senate. A member of the Senate needs to be five years older, have been a citizen for two years longer, and serves a term that's four years longer than that of a member of the House. The Founders thought of the Senate as a more elite group, which accounts for the differences and why they wanted Senators to serve longer terms.

Section 4

The Section 4 of Article I simply says that each state will control its own elections, but that Congress has the right to change voting regulations by law. It also declares that Congress should assemble at least once per year.

Section 5

Section 5 describes that the rules for the proceedings in Congress should be regulated by Congress and that a journal, or record, should be kept of those proceedings. Every so often the record should be published, although items that "require secrecy" can be left out. Also, a majority of each house needs to be present in order to conduct official business, but smaller groups can meet on a day-to-day basis.

PRACTICE 1

For the following, write the section number of the appropriate Section (**1–5**) of Article I on the line provided.

1. The states will control their own elections. __________

2. The vice president is the president of the Senate. __________

3. A member of the House of Representatives must be at least 25 years old. __________

4. Congress will consist of two houses, the Senate and the House of Representatives. __________

5. To become a senator, a person must have been a citizen of the United States for at least nine years. __________

6. A slave was considered three-fifths of a person for purposes of the population count. __________

7. Congress should keep a record of its proceedings. __________

8. The number of members representing each state in the House of Representatives is based on the population of the state. __________

9. There will be two senators from each state. __________

10. A member of the House of Representatives serves a two-year term. __________

ANSWERS

1. Section 4
2. Section 3
3. Section 2
4. Section 1
5. Section 3
6. Section 2
7. Section 5
8. Section 2
9. Section 3
10. Section 2

Section 6

The next section, Section 6, lays down three more rules involving the Congress: (1) members of Congress will be paid by the Treasury of the United States; (2) except for crimes of "Treason, Felony and Breach of the Peace," members cannot be arrested while attending a session of Congress or on their way to and from that session; and (3) if a person is elected to Congress he or she cannot also be appointed to another position within the government and vice versa. For instance, a person cannot be the president's secretary and a Congressperson at the same time.

Section 7

Ever wonder how a bill becomes a law?

DEFINITION A bill is a draft of a law.

Well, Section 7 explains the whole process. (Although, first it starts off by declaring that all bills involving the raising of money will originate in the House of Representatives.) A bill is proposed by a member of either the Senate or the House of Representatives. If the bill is approved by a majority vote in whichever house proposes it, it then moves on to the other house for approval. If both the Senate and the House of Representatives approve the bill, then it goes to the president. At this time the president has 10 days to either sign the bill, in which case it becomes a law, or return it to Congress with his objections. If he returns it to Congress unsigned, two-thirds of each house must consider the President's objections to approve it. Then it's a law. If the President fails to either sign the bill into law or return it to Congress within the ten-day window, it automatically becomes a law.

Section 8

In Section 8 the Founders listed the powers that were given to Congress. Here are some highlights of the list. Congress can

- Collect taxes.
- Borrow money.
- Regulate commerce.
- Coin money.
- Establish post offices.
- Declare war.
- Provide, maintain, and support armies and a navy.
- Provide punishment for the counterfeiting of money.

Section 9

Section 9 is one of the more significant rules having to do with slavery. It states that the "Importation of such Persons as any of the States now existing shall think proper to admit" would not be prohibited until the year 1808 (which, when the Constitution was written, was 21 years in the future). This was part of another compromise, since some southern states were concerned that the Constitution would abolish the slave trade. Some delegates who participated in the debates were against slave importation, so they decided that for 21 years, states would retain control of the issue and that Congress could ban slave imports after that.

More of Section 9 discusses rules and regulations related to the Treasury. For instance, Section 9 says that accounts of public money should be published every now and then, and that there would be no taxes on states' exports. Section 9 also states that the legislative branch can't punish people for crimes without a trial or pass any law that changes the consequences of actions committed before the passing of that law.

Section 10

Section 10 of Article I of the Constitution bans the states from doing several things, such as coining money, entering into treaties, and granting titles of nobility. It also says that states cannot tax imports without Congress's consent, engage in war, or maintain an army in peacetime.

PRACTICE 2

For the following, write on the line provided the number of the appropriate Section (**6–10**) of Article I.

1. The international slave trade will not be prohibited for 20 years.
____

2. A member of Congress cannot be arrested for certain crimes while they are on the job. __________

3. States do not have the powers that Congress has. __________

4. Congress can borrow money. __________

5. The president has ten days to either sign a bill or send it back to Congress. __________

6. Congress can declare war. __________

7. Members of Congress will be paid by the U.S. Treasury. __________

8. Accounts of public money should occasionally be published. __________

9. Two-thirds of each house must re-approve a bill for it to become a law. __________

10. Congress can collect taxes. __________

ANSWERS

1. **Section 9**
2. **Section 6**
3. **Section 10**
4. **Section 8**
5. **Section 7**
6. **Section 8**
7. **Section 6**
8. **Section 9**
9. **Section 7**
10. **Section 8**

LESSON 7

articles ii–vii

Justice, sir, is the great interest of man on earth.
—DANIEL WEBSTER

This lesson continues to explain the Articles of the Constitution, focusing on Articles II through VII. You'll learn the specifics of the rules and regulations that the Founders decided would form the basis of our government.

IN THE PREVIOUS lesson you learned all about the first article of the Constitution. Now let's move on to the rest of the articles.

ARTICLE II

The second article of the Constitution is divided into four sections and discusses some rules and regulations related to the presidency. First, in Section 1, the Founders state that the executive power in the government will belong to the president, who will serve a four-year term along with the vice president. Also, the president must have been born in the United States, have lived in the country for at least 14 years, and be at least thirty-five years old.

Section 1 then goes on to explain the system for electing the president, which is known as the **Electoral College**. This is how it works. Each state gets a certain number of electors. That number is equal to the number of the state's senators plus the number of the state's representatives. Each elector votes for two people for president. The person who receives the greatest number of votes becomes the president and the person who receives the second greatest becomes the vice president. Even though certain parts of the electoral system have changed, the president is still not elected directly by the people.

FUN FACT As you probably know, in presidential elections today the presidential candidate chooses a person to run with him or her as the vice presidential candidate. The two of them run as a *ticket* or team.

In Section 2 of Article II, we learn that the president will be the commander-in-chief of the armed forces and also about some of the powers given to the office of the presidency. We learn that the president can make treaties as long as two-thirds of the senate agrees. The president also has the power to appoint ambassadors, other high executive branch officials, and federal judges, as long as a majority of senators agree.

DEFINITION An *ambassador* is a person who is appointed to officially represent his or her country while living in that country.

Section 3 requires that the president let Congress know "Information of the State of the Union" every now and then, which means that the president should keep Congress informed about how the country is doing. Finally, Section 4 says that Congress can remove from office either the president or the vice president if they commit treason, bribery or any "other high Crimes and Misdemeanors."

ARTICLE III

Article III of the Constitution discusses the country's judicial system and begins in Section 1 by decreeing that judicial power of the United States belongs to the Supreme Court. Section 2 then lists the sorts of cases to which the federal judicial power will extend. It also states that all trials (except impeachment trials) will have a jury and will take place in the state where the crime was committed.

The Founders devoted all of Section 3 of Article III to the subject of **treason**, which they defined as warring against the United States or aiding any enemies of the United States. For a person to be convicted of treason, there must be two witnesses to the act or the accused traitor must confess in open court to his or her crimes.

ARTICLE IV

Article IV of the Constitution is all about the states. Section 1 indicates that all states must accept the proceedings of other states and Section 2 says that citizens of each state should be treated to the same privileges of citizens in other states. Also, an accused criminal cannot flee a trial by going to another state. If caught, the accused criminal will be returned for trial in the state in which the crime was committed.

At the time the Constitution was written, there were only 13 states, but the Founders were well aware of all the land out west and made regulations for admitting other states into the union. Section 3 of Article IV says that new states can be added if approved by Congress, but that no state can be formed entirely within an existing state without that state's permission. Also, Congress has power over the rules and regulations of all territories that are not states.

The last section of Article IV declares that every state will be protected from invasion and from domestic violence. In other words, the federal government will step in to prevent uprising within a state and any invasion of a state.

ARTICLE V

Article V is an important part of the Constitution as you will see in the rest of this book. It's all about making amendments to the Constitution. The Founders realized in order to be fair and to accommodate changing sentiments, they had to make the Constitution a flexible document. So, this is what they decided.

Congress can make amendments to the Constitution. A proposal for a new amendment can be submitted by either two-thirds of both houses of Congress or the legislatures of two-thirds of the states. In order to ratify a new amendment and make it official, it must be ratified either by the legislatures of three-fourths of the states, or by special conventions in three-fourths of the states.

Article V also spells out some rules regarding what kind of amendments can be added. For instance, there can't be an amendment that takes away a state's vote in the Senate. And do you remember what it says in Section 9 of Article I? It says that the international slave trade cannot be abolished before 1808. So, Article V agrees that until 1808, there can't be an amendment that affects the first and fourth parts of Section 9, Article I.

ARTICLE VI

This article serves as sort of a wrap-up. It lays down the law about the document that has just been created. First, it states that all debts that existed before the ratification of the Constitution will carry over. So, just because there is a new document establishing a new system of government doesn't mean that debts are no longer owed. Then Article VI declares that the Constitution and laws made under it are the "supreme law of the Land." All members of all branches of the government are bound by oath to support the Constitution, and religion will never be a factor in determining if a person is qualified for any office within the government.

ACTIVITY Why do you think that the Founders put in a line about religion not being a factor in a person holding a government office?

ARTICLE VII

Now we've come to the last article of the Constitution. This is the last bit of writing that the Founders put down before the document was ratified. According to this article, nine states must ratify the document for the Constitution to take effect. It is following Article VII that some of the Founding Fathers (state delegates) signed and dated the Constitution. It's dated September 17, 1787.

PRACTICE 1

For each of the following phrases, write the *article* number and *section* number to which the phrase most closely refers. If an article doesn't have any sections, just leave the space blank.

1. New states can be added to the Union.
Article _____ Section _____

2. Nine states must ratify the Constitution.
Article _____ Section _____

3. The president is the commander-in-chief of the armed forces.
Article _____ Section _____

4. The president serves a four-year term.
Article _____ Section _____

5. Accused criminals who are caught across state lines will be returned for trial in the state in which the crime was committed.
Article _____ Section _____

6. Members of the government must take an oath to support the Constitution.
Article _____ Section _____

7. Judicial power belongs to the Supreme Court.
Article _____ Section _____

8. State electors = # of senators + # of representatives.
Article _____ Section _____

9. Trials will have a jury.
Article _____ Section _____

10. Amendments to the Constitution can be made.
Article _____ Section _____

11. The president can appoint ambassadors.
Article _____ Section _____

12. The president will let Congress know the state of the union.
Article _____ Section _____

13. No one can amend the Constitution to take away a state's vote in the senate.
Article _____ Section _____

14. Congress decides the punishment for treason.
Article _____ Section _____

15. States are protected from invasion.
Article _____ Section _____

ANSWERS

1. **Article IV, Section 3**
2. **Article VII**
3. **Article II, Section 2**
4. **Article II, Section 1**
5. **Article IV, Section 2**
6. **Article VI**
7. **Article III, Section 1**
8. **Article II, Section 1**
9. **Article III, Section 2**
10. **Article V**
11. **Article II, Section 2**
12. **Article II, Section 3**
13. **Article V**
14. **Article III, Section 3**
15. **Article IV, Section 4**

SECTION 3
the bill of rights

LESSON 8

the first amendment

The Constitution does not just protect those whose views we share; it also protects those with whose views we disagree.

—Edward Kennedy

This lesson introduces you to the Bill of Rights and the First Amendment in particular. First, we review the origin of the Bill of Rights and discuss who interprets the Constitution. Then we will dive right into the First Amendment and find out what it's all about.

REMEMBER BACK IN Lesson 4 when we learned about the Federalists and the Anti-Federalists? Maybe you remember that one of the problems the Anti-Federalists had when it came to ratifying the Constitution was that they felt it didn't do enough to secure some basic rights for citizens. In order to convince these opponents of ratification to hop on board, Federalists promised that as soon as the Constitution was ratified, Congress would send a proposed bill of rights to the states for their ratification. That **Bill of Rights** is the first ten amendments (additions) to the Constitution, and as you'll see in the coming lessons, it does a lot to secure those rights the Anti-Federalists wanted.

INTERPRETING THE CONSTITUTION

Before we begin talking about the amendments and the First Amendment in particular, let's take a moment to think about how the Constitution is used on a day-to-day basis in our country. It will be helpful for you, as you learn about the amendments, to consider just who is looking to these amendments for guidance and under what circumstances those people are interpreting the Constitution.

You probably don't think much about the Constitution in your life. Most of us just go about our business and take for granted all the rights and liberties that the document bestows on us as citizens. But there are some people who make it their job to think about and interpret the Constitution. For instance, a judge might have to decide a case based on a Constitutional issue. Did so-and-so have the *right* to do what he or she did? Is a person's right to do such-and-such protected by the Constitution? These are questions a judge might have to answer. It is the job of the judicial system to read the Constitution and its amendments in search of answers to these questions. Similarly, before a member of Congress votes for a bill and before a president signs one, it is their job to ask whether it is constitutional as well. State officials have the same responsibility, as they take an oath to uphold it, too. Keep this in mind as you go through the rest of this book.

THE FIRST AMENDMENT

The First Amendment secures freedom of religion, speech, press, assembly, and petition. This is how it is written.

> *Congress shall make no law respecting an establishment of religion, or prohibiting the free exercise thereof; or abridging the freedom of speech, or of the press; or the right of the people peaceably to assemble, and to petition the Government for a redress of grievances.*

If you read closely, each phrase in the amendment refers to a protection given to citizens of the United States. Let's look at the amendment phrase by phrase.

> *Congress shall make no law respecting an establishment of religion*

What this means is that Congress is not allowed to pass a law that makes a certain religion the official religion of the country. Some of the people who lived during the time the Constitution was created had come to the United States to flee religious persecution in another country. The Founding Fathers wanted to make sure that the federal government could never take away a person's freedom to practice whatever religion he or she chose. They also wanted to protect the established churches in several states from federal interference. This brings us to the next phrase, which reads:

Or prohibiting the free exercise thereof

In other words, Congress cannot pass a law prohibiting the practicing of a religion.

Here is the next phrase of the First Amendment:

Or abridging the freedom of speech

This one seems pretty self-explanatory. Congress cannot pass a law that interferes with citizens' rights to speak freely. But, as you'll see throughout the rest of this book, throughout our country's history there have been times (and there will continue to be times) when officials had to interpret what the Constitution says. Although, according to the Constitution, a citizen is given this freedom of speech, sometimes there are exceptions. For instance, it is against the law to yell "Fire!" in a crowded theater if you know there is no fire. This is because it puts people in danger. Think about it. What would happen if a person yelled "Fire!" in a crowded theater? People would panic and it's likely that someone would get hurt in the midst of that panic.

DEFINITION While the First Amendment does protect your freedom of speech, you are not allowed to make false accusations about somebody if it will damage his or her reputation. This is called *slander.*

So, as you can see, while *freedom of speech* seems like a simple enough protection in the Bill of Rights, there are often complications that arise when we start to look at real-life, common sense scenarios involving those rights.

The next phrase is:

Or of the press

Congress cannot pass a law that prevents people from being able to print what they want. You might notice that this is a form of freedom of speech, only applied to print material, like magazines and newspapers.

ACTIVITY Imagine you're the editor of the school newspaper and that you weren't allowed to print anything negative about your school. Write a paragraph or two about the effect this rule would have on you and your fellow students.

The First Amendment also protects citizens' right to peaceful assembly. This is what it says.

> *Or the right of the people peaceably to assemble*

Notice that the word *peaceably* is added in there and it isn't just *the right of the people to assemble.* Peaceful assembly is protected under the First Amendment, but not violent assembly, which is more like a riot, where people might get hurt.

The last phrase of the First Amendment refers to petitioning.

> *And to petition the Government for a redress of grievances*

What this means is that if the citizens of the country disagree with something the government is doing, they have the right to ask the government to fix whatever they think is wrong. A "petition" is a request. To "redress" is to make right and "grievances" are things you would find reason to complain about. So, "to petition the Government for a redress of grievances" is to request that the government make right something you think is worthy of complaint.

PRACTICE 1

Decide whether each of the following statements is *true* or *false* and write it on the line provided.

1. The Constitution allows you to say whatever you want. _______

2. The Amendments are so clear that no interpretation is needed. _______

3. The First Amendment secures freedom of the press. _______

4. The first 10 amendments were added immediately after ratification. _______

5. The First Amendment guarantees freedom of speech. _______

6. Officials take an oath to uphold the Constitution. _______

7. Our Founding Fathers were unconcerned with religion. _______

8. The Anti-Federalists wanted a Bill of Rights. _______

9. The Bill of Rights is the first 12 amendments. _______

10. Congress cannot establish an official religion. _______

11. Women's right to vote is secured by the First Amendment. _______

12. Judges decide if a person's rights have been interfered with. _______

13. Grievances are things you are happy about. _______

14. The First Amendment is part of the Bill of Rights. _______

15. I have the right to gather with my friends in a public park and have a peaceful discussion. _______

ANSWERS

1. **false.** Even though the First Amendment guarantees freedom of speech, there are still exceptions, like saying something with the knowledge that it could cause physical harm to people.
2. **false.** It is true that the Amendments are fairly simply stated, but in some cases this leaves them open to interpretation by judges and Constitutional scholars.
3. **true.** The First Amendment does secure freedom of the press.
4. **true.** James Madison promised the Anti-Federalists that a Bill of Rights would be added immediately after ratification, and he kept his promise.
5. **true.** The First Amendment guarantees freedom of speech.

6. **false.** Judges look to the Constitution all the time to determine if people's rights have been violated.
7. **false.** The Founders were concerned that religious freedom could be taken away, which is why in the First Amendment they stated that Congress could not either establish an official religion or prohibit people from practicing whatever religion they chose.
8. **true.** The Anti-Federalists were concerned that the Constitution as it was did not protect the basic rights of the citizens. They wanted a Bill of Rights to be included.
9. **false.** The Bill of Rights is the first 10 amendments.
10. **true.** The First Amendment prohibits Congress from establishing an official religion.
11. **false.** Women's right to vote is not mentioned in the First Amendment. The Nineteenth Amendment secures the right for women to vote.
12. **true.** Part of a judge's job is to determine if a person's rights have been violated.
13. **false.** Grievances are things you have a complaint about.
14. **true.** The Bill of Rights is the first 10 amendments of the Constitution, so the First Amendment is part of the Bill of Rights.
15. **true.** The First Amendment guarantees the right to peaceful assembly.

LESSON 9

the second amendment

The Constitution should never be construed . . . to prevent the people of the United States who are peaceable citizens from keeping their own arms.

—Samuel Adams

This lesson discusses the meaning of the Second Amendment of the Constitution, as well as the debate that surrounds it. You will learn about why the Founders might have written this particular amendment and about today's differing sides of the gun control discussion as it relates to the Second Amendment.

HAVE YOU EVER heard people discussing the topic of gun control or been part of a discussion yourself? It's been a hot topic in our country's media and political debates. Now you will discover the origin of the debate. It all comes back to the Second Amendment, which is one of the most famous and talked about of all 27 amendments.

First, let's take a look at the exact wording of the amendment.

A well regulated Militia, being necessary to the security of a free State, the right of the people to keep and bear Arms, shall not be infringed.

Now, since sometimes the language they used back then can be difficult to understand, it's helpful to re-phrase the amendment using more modern language. Basically, what the amendment is saying is this:

Given that a militia is needed for the security of a free state, people will always have the right to be equipped with "Arms."

(You'll notice that the word *Arms* is the same as the original text.)

DEFINITION To *bear* means to be equipped with.

After reading this new, modern language version of the Second Amendment, there seems to be an implied phrase at the end that brings the meaning into clearer focus.

> *Given that a militia is needed for the security of a free state, people will always have the right to have "Arms,"* ***so that it is possible for them to form a militia.***

This brings us to the term *militia*. You might be thinking, What exactly is a militia? Why was it so important back then? Clearly, the Founding Fathers felt that a militia was necessary for security purposes.

A **militia** is a group of citizens who get together to perform military services. It's a citizen army. Today we have National Guard (state militia) and the U.S. Army, which is operated by our federal government. But that wasn't always the case. When the American Revolution was just beginning and the colonists began to resist the British, they had no professional army to back them up. They had to take matters into their own hands, whether to protect themselves from the increasingly aggressive British soldiers or to assert their new feelings of independence.

In April 1775 the first official battle of the Revolutionary War was fought at Lexington, near Boston. It was a battle between British soldiers and a militia formed by colonists in the area. When word of the fighting reached Philadelphia, the Second Continental Congress decided they needed to have a centralized government, including an army. They formed the Continental Army and appointed George Washington to be its commander.

So, you can see that in 1787, when the Constitution was written, it hadn't been very long since the colonists had had to rely on militias to fight the British. Therefore, it's not very surprising that the Founding Fathers wrote the Second Amendment about the right to "keep and bear Arms."

THE DEBATE

Now you know a little bit about the Second Amendment's origins. Let's take a look at the debate about the amendment that continues today. There are really just two sides to the discussion. On one side, there are people who believe that the Second Amendment should be interpreted strictly and literally. On the other side, there are people who believe that since our country is so different from what it was like when our Founding Fathers were writing the Constitution, we need to think about what they meant and how we might apply that to today's society.

Strict Interpretation

Those who favor a strict interpretation of the Second Amendment make the argument that since it says in the Constitution that citizens of the United States have the "right to keep and bear Arms," the government cannot prevent them from the opportunity to buy and house guns. After all, they might argue, if it's important to uphold and protect other rights given to us by the Constitution and the Bill of Rights in particular (like freedom of speech and freedom of religion), then why should this be any different?

Liberal Interpretation

Those in favor of a more liberal, or less-strict, interpretation of the Second Amendment argue that the right to bear arms is, in fact, different from other rights guaranteed by the Constitution. First, they argue that the Second Amendment was written in a time when it was necessary to maintain the citizens' ability to form militias for their own security. And forming a militia can be accomplished only if citizens have the right to obtain and keep weapons with which to fight. Since, at this time we have a professional military, the Founders' intention no longer has bearing. Also, it could be argued that just as you're not allowed to yell "Fire!" in a crowded theater if you know there is no fire (even though your freedom of speech is protected by the First Amendment), because doing so might put people in harm's way, keeping guns around could also put people in harm's way.

There's also the issue of what the Founders meant by the word "Arms." In a general sense, *arms* are weapons. In today's debate about the Second Amendment, what everyone talks about is guns, the right to keep and bear guns. It is true that those colonial militia men fighting at Lexington were using guns—although they were using muskets, not the handguns and automatic weapons that we see in real-life situations.

ACTIVITY Think about which interpretation of the Second Amendment you favor. Then write a letter to your senator explaining why you think the amendment should be interpreted the way you favor.

Isn't it interesting how something written by people more than 200 years ago can be so hotly debated today? We will never really know what the Founders meant by what they said. One thing we do know is that it was a hot debate in 1787 too. As you learned in Lesson 3, the Founders didn't always agree, either. They were just trying to do the right thing for their brand new country. The Second Amendment, or the right to keep and bear arms, is one of the shortest amendments. It's just one short sentence. But that one short sentence has been pulled apart, dissected, and analyzed by many people over the years.

PRACTICE 1

Use the following words or phrases to fill in the blanks for questions **1–10**. Some may be used more than once.

arms	militia	debate
Continental Army	British	
Continental Congress	Founders	
Bunker Hill	liberal	
bear	gun control	

1. A well regulated __________, being necessary to the security of a free State, the right of the people to keep and bear __________, shall not be infringed.

2. Delegates at the ______________ heard about the fighting at ______________ and decided to form the ______________.

3. A strict interpretation of the Second Amendment is one that defends our right to keep and __________ arms.

4. George Washington was commander of the ______________.

5. The Second Amendment has been the topic of much ________.

6. The citizens got together to form a __________.

7. A __________ interpretation of the Second Amendment is one that argues that we no longer have a need for a __________, so therefore we don't need the right to bear __________.

8. The Battle of ______________ was fought between __________ soldiers and colonists.

9. We will never really know what the ________________ meant when they wrote the Constitution.

10. People refer to the Second Amendment when they are arguing about __________.

ANSWERS

1. A well regulated **militia**, being necessary to the security of a free State, the right of the people to keep and bear **arms**, shall not be infringed.
2. Delegates at the **Continental Congress** heard about the fighting at **Bunker Hill** and decided to form the **Continental Army**.
3. A strict interpretation of the Second Amendment is one that defends our right to keep and **bear** arms.
4. George Washington was commander of the **Continental Army**.
5. The Second Amendment has been the topic of much **debate**.
6. The citizens got together to form a **militia**.
7. A **liberal** interpretation of the Second Amendment is one that argues that we no longer have a need for a **militia**, so therefore don't need the right to bear **arms**.
8. The Battle of **Bunker Hill** was fought between **British** soldiers and colonists.
9. We will never really know what the **Founders** meant when they wrote the Constitution.
10. People refer to the Second Amendment when they're arguing about **gun control**.

LESSON 10

the third and fourth amendments

When a man assumes a public trust,
he should consider himself as public property.
—THOMAS JEFFERSON

This lesson discusses the Third and Fourth Amendments to the Constitution. It will explain what each amendment means and will give some information about why they are included in the Bill of Rights, including why, if at all, they are relevant today.

BOTH THE THIRD and Fourth Amendments to the Constitution concern citizens' homes and property, but in two different ways. One deals with the housing of soldiers and the other with searches and seizures.

THE THIRD ADMENDMENT

Let's take a closer look at the Third Amendment. Here is how it was written.

> *No Soldier shall, in time of peace be quartered in any house, without the consent of the Owner, nor in time of war, but in a manner to be prescribed by law.*

Basically, what the Third Amendment says is that citizens have the right NOT to let soldiers sleep or eat in their houses. Only in a time of war, if Congress makes a relevant law, would a person have to house or feed a soldier. Of course, the amendment states, an owner *could* consent to housing and/or feeding a soldier, but the owner has the right to refuse to do so.

Now you're probably thinking, when is this relevant? When would a soldier ever need to sleep or eat in a citizen's home? Well, that's a very good question. Today the United States has a large army, equipped with bases that include housing for soldiers and places for those soldiers to eat. But back in 1787, when the Constitution was written, things were very different.

In 1774, Parliament had adopted a Quartering Act empowering British military officers to house British soldiers in citizens' private buildings. American colonists feared they might have to house soldiers in their homes. You can see why the Anti-Federalists wanted an amendment guaranteeing that the federal government would never make citizens house soldiers in peacetime, either.

ACTIVITY Take a minute to think about how you might feel about soldiers eating and sleeping in your home. Decide whether you think the Third Amendment is necessary and then write a short paragraph explaining your decision.

PRACTICE 1

Write the letter of the best answer for the following questions.

1. Under what circumstance is a soldier allowed to sleep in a citizen's home?

- **a.** There's nowhere else to sleep.
- **b.** The citizen allows it.
- **c.** The government says so.
- **d.** none of the above

2. It is a citizen's right to

- **a.** let a soldier eat dinner with the citizen's family.
- **b.** refuse to let a soldier sleep in the house.
- **c.** invite a soldier to lunch in his or her home.
- **d.** all of the above

3. What is a *militia*?
   a. the able-bodied male citizenry of military age trained to arms
   b. a bunch of naval officers
   c. a kind of gun
   d. a formal army

4. Why did the Founding Fathers include the Third Amendment?
   a. They wanted to make sure soldiers had enough to eat.
   b. They wanted to make sure soldiers had housing.
   c. They didn't want citizens to feel burdened by soldiers.
   d. They wanted to do away with militias.

5. When was the Continental Army formed?
   a. just before the Battle of Lexington
   b. during the Second Continental Congress
   c. after the Constitution had been ratified
   d. when the Third Amendment was written

ANSWERS

1. **b.** According to the Third Amendment, a soldier can sleep in a citizen's home only if the citizen allows it.
2. **d.** A citizen has the right to either invite a soldier in or refuse to do so.
3. **a.** A *militia* is the able-bodied male citizenry of military age trained to arms.
4. **c.** The Founders wanted to make sure that citizens had the right to not allow soldiers in their home.
5. **b.** The Continental Army was formed during the Second Continental Congress.

THE FOURTH AMENDMENT

Ever watch any police dramas on television? If so, you're probably already familiar with some of the rules laid out in the Fourth Amendment. It deals with the issue of searches and seizures of citizen's property. This is the text of the amendment.

The right of the people to be secure in their persons, houses, papers, and effects, against unreasonable searches and seizures, shall not be violated and no Warrants shall issue, but upon probable cause, supported by Oath or affirmation, and particularly describing the place to be searched, and the persons or things to be seized.

Let's break it down into smaller pieces to uncover its meaning. The first part of the amendment states that people, homes, and property cannot be searched or taken away unless a certain procedure is followed according to the law. This is the part that says

The right of the people to be secure in their persons, houses, papers, and effects, against unreasonable searches and seizures, shall not be violated

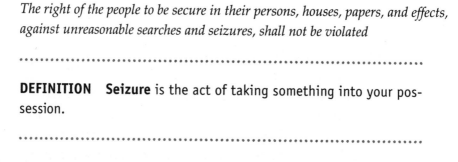

DEFINITION **Seizure** is the act of taking something into your possession.

The second section of the Fourth Amendment explains the procedure that must be followed when a person, house, or property is either searched or taken away.

no Warrants shall issue, but upon probable cause, supported by Oath or affirmation, and particularly describing the place to be searched, and the persons or things to be seized.

First, it might be helpful to know what a *warrant* is. In this case, it is a document issued by a court that gives permission to do something. So, this second section of the Fourth Amendment says that a court cannot give permission to conduct a search or take any person or evidence without "probable cause." In other words, there has to be a good reason. The warrant also has to be "supported by Oath or affirmation," which means the person giving the reason must promise to be telling the truth. The person asking for the warrant must also describe the place that he or she wishes to search. Also, before a warrant giving permission to take (arrest) a person or seize property is served, the person asking for the warrant must specify which person or what property he or she wishes to take.

Essentially, these are the two points to remember about the Fourth Amendment.

1. People, homes, and property cannot be taken away or searched without a warrant.

2. To obtain a warrant you must
   a. have a good reason.
   b. promise you are telling the truth.
   c. describe where the search will take place.
   d. if you are taking something or someone, describe what or who is to be taken.

ACTIVITY Choose a room in an acquaintance's house that you would like a warrant to search. Write a brief proposal for a warrant, making sure to include all the essential information. Describe the room. Explain your good reason for wanting to search the room and if you will be taking something from the room, describe the thing you will be taking and why.

PRACTICE 2

Put the letters of the following situations in the correct column according to the rules of the Fourth Amendment.

a. Police want to search a home without a warrant.
b. Police arrest Sally Jones after getting a warrant from a judge.
c. Police want a warrant to arrest someone, but can't describe or name him.
d. Police want to obtain a warrant to search a house, but can't describe what they are looking for.
e. Police show up at a home with a warrant to search for a specific item.

Allowed	Not Allowed

ANSWERS

Allowed	Not Allowed
b	a
e	c
	d

According to the Fourth Amendment, police officers are allowed to arrest someone if they have a warrant, and they are allowed to search someone's home if they have a warrant to look for a specific item. They are not allowed to search a home without a warrant, obtain an arrest warrant for an unidentified person, or obtain a search warrant for an unidentified item.

LESSON 11

the fifth amendment

A bill of rights is what the people are entitled to against every government on earth, general or particular, and what no just government should refuse, or rest on inferences.

—Thomas Jefferson

This lesson explains the Fifth Amendment of the Constitution. It discusses the rights given by the amendment having to do with life, liberty, and property, and focuses on some familiar phrases, like *grand jury* and *pleading the Fifth*.

YOU'VE SEEN IN the previous few lessons that the Bill of Rights (those first ten amendments) focuses on some basic rights that the Founders felt should not be taken away. The Fifth Amendment continues the theme by focusing on some basic rights having to due with life, liberty, and property. Here is the amendment:

> *No person shall be held to answer for a capital, or otherwise infamous crime, unless on a presentment or indictment of a Grand Jury, except in cases arising in the land or naval forces, or in the Militia, when in actual service in time of war or public danger; nor shall any person be subject for the same offence to be twice put in jeopardy of life or limb; nor shall be compelled in any Criminal Case to be a witness against himself, nor be deprived of life, liberty, or property, without due process of law; nor shall private property be taken for public use without just compensation.*

Since this is such a long amendment, it will be helpful to break it down into smaller pieces in order to understand its meaning. We'll start with the first part.

> *No person shall be held to answer for a capital, or otherwise infamous crime, unless on a presentment or indictment of a Grand Jury*

This part says that before a person can be put on trial for a serious crime, he or she must first go before a **Grand Jury**, which is a special jury that decides if there is enough evidence or reason for there to be a trial.

DEFINITION A **capital** crime is a crime for which the punishment is death.

There is an exception, however.

> *except in cases arising in the land or naval forces, or in the Militia, when in actual service in time of war or public danger*

A grand jury decision is not necessary in cases involving members of the military, if they are in service during a time of war or "public danger."

What a grand jury does is to act as a first step in the trial process when it comes to serious crimes. Why do you think the Founders decided to add this extra step? They could just have said that anyone accused of a serious crime would go to trial and that would be that. Why the extra step?

As we discussed previously, we will never know exactly what the Founders were thinking. All we can do is think about what makes sense. The extra step in the process makes it more difficult to convict a person for a serious crime. You can't just go around accusing people of horrific acts and then have that person stand trial for it. Imagine if someone accused you of a serious crime that you had not committed. You wouldn't want to have to stand trial. You would want for your accuser to have to prove that they have enough evidence against you to make their accusation reasonable. So, the grand jury protects citizens from having to stand trial when there is not enough evidence to support an accusation of guilt.

Now, onto the next piece of the Fifth Amendment. Does the term *double jeopardy* sound familiar to you? If so, you might already have an idea what this piece of the amendment is about.

nor shall any person be subject for the same offence to be twice put in jeopardy of life or limb

What this means is that a person cannot be tried twice for the same crime. Today, it is commonly referred to as **double jeopardy**.

You might also be familiar with the next part of the Fifth Amendment. It says:

nor shall be compelled in any criminal case to be a witness against himself

Have you ever heard about someone *pleading the fifth*? Well, *the fifth* refers to the Fifth Amendment and to this part of the amendment in particular. The Fifth Amendment says that a citizen has the right NOT to testify against himself or incriminate himself by saying something. So instead of sitting in court and admitting to something that might be evidence of your guilt, you are allowed to **plead the fifth**, or not say anything.

Some other rights are spelled out in the next piece of the amendment.

nor be deprived of life, liberty, or property, without due process of law

This part is pretty straightforward. A person's life, freedom, or property cannot be taken away from him or her without going through due process of the law.

Implied in this last part of the amendment is that the government is allowed to seize private property for public use, but it cannot do it without justly compensating the citizen.

nor shall private property be taken for public use without just compensation

Maybe you're wondering how the government would be allowed to take private property for public use. Think about our highway system today. Think about all the public roads that crisscross the country. At some time, the property on which those roads sit was privately owned. Imagine how difficult it would be to create a highway between two cities if a citizen halfway down the road wouldn't give up his or her property. This is why it is sometimes necessary for the government to take over private property. The Fifth Amendment makes sure that the citizen is offered a fair price.

DEFINITION Have you ever heard the term **eminent domain**? Eminent domain is what is implied by the Fifth Amendment. It is the right of the government to take private property for public use, such as a state highway or an international airport.

PRACTICE 1

Match each of the following phrases with the corresponding phrase in the next column.

1. capital crime	**a.** can't testify against yourself
2. grand jury	**b.** tried twice for the same crime
3. double jeopardy	**c.** private property taken for public use
4. plead the fifth	**d.** death penalty
5. eminent domain	**e.** one step before a trial

Decide whether the following statements are *true* or *false*.

6. The government can seize public land without compensating the owner.

7. Life, liberty, and property are all protected under the Fifth Amendment.

8. I have the right to keep quiet if something I say in court might make me look guilty.

9. Grand juries act as a safeguard to protect guilty citizens.

10. Grand juries deal only with civil (not criminal) cases.

ANSWERS

1. **d**
2. **e**
3. **b**
4. **a**
5. **c**
6. **false.** The government can seize private land for public use only if the government fairly compensates the owner of that land.
7. **true.**
8. **true.**
9. **false.** Grand juries serve as a protection of rights for all citizens.
10. **false.** Grand juries deal only with serious or capital crimes, not civil cases.

LESSON 12

the sixth, seventh, and eighth amendments

I consider trial by jury as the only anchor ever yet imagined by man, by which a government can be held to the principles of its constitution.

—THOMAS JEFFERSON

This lesson considers some of the rights of citizens who are accused of crimes—specifically, those dealt with in the Sixth, Seventh, and Eighth Amendments to the Constitution. Each of the three amendments are explained, and we discuss why they were included by the Founders in the Bill of Rights.

IMAGINE BEING ACCUSED of a crime in a country that did not protect the rights of accused citizens. You might not be informed about what crime you were supposed to have committed, or even get to confront your accusers. You might be kept in jail waiting for a trial that never seems to happen. You might not have access to a lawyer to defend you. The Constitution and the Sixth, Seventh, and Eighth Amendments of the Bill of Rights specifically protect your rights as a citizen, if you are ever accused of a crime.

SIXTH AMENDMENT

First, let's take a look at what the Sixth Amendment says.

In all criminal prosecutions, the accused shall enjoy the right to a speedy and public trial, by an impartial jury of the State and district wherein the crime shall have been committed, which district shall have been previously

> *ascertained by law and to be informed of the nature and cause of the accusation; to be confronted with the witnesses against him; to have compulsory process for obtaining witnesses in his favor, and to have the assistance of counsel for his defense.*

You can tell from the first phrase that this amendment deals with the rights of people who are accused in criminal cases. These are the rights guaranteed by the Sixth Amendment.

- Right to a speedy trial
- Right to a public trial
- Right to a fair jury
- Right to be told of what he or she is being accused
- Right to face witnesses who are testifying against the accused
- Right to present witnesses who will testify in favor of the accused
- Right to a lawyer

In addition to these rights, the Sixth Amendment specifies that the trial must take place in the state and district where the crime was alleged to have occurred.

Some people might think, Why did the Founders go to all the trouble to protect the rights of criminals? But remember, not everyone who is accused of a crime is guilty. The reason that the judicial system exists is to attempt to find out the truth. If the Sixth Amendment had not been included, it would have been much easier for an innocent person to find themselves in a situation where they had no opportunity for the truth to be uncovered.

ACTIVITY Take a minute to think about how you would feel if you were accused of a crime you hadn't committed. Write a letter to one of the Founding Fathers explaining your thoughts about the Sixth Amendment.

SEVENTH AMENDMENT

Unlike the Sixth Amendment, which deals with criminal cases, the Seventh Amendment deals with civil cases or "suits at common law." This is what the amendment says:

In suits at common law, where the value in controversy shall exceed twenty dollars, the right of trial by jury shall be preserved, and no fact tried by a jury, shall be otherwise reexamined in any Court of the United States, than according to the rules of the common law.

In civil cases, where the dollar amount involved is more than $20, the accused party has the **right** to a **jury trial**. Also, the ruling of that jury will not be reexamined by any other court in the country except according to the rules of civil cases. Keep in mind, however, that when the Bill of Rights was drafted $20 was worth a lot more than it is today.

EIGHTH AMENDMENT

This amendment is very straightforward. It states three rules regarding people accused of crimes.

Excessive bail shall not be required, nor excessive fines imposed, nor cruel and unusual punishments inflicted.

The first rule is this. An accused person has the right to a fair bail. In other words, the amount of bail should be reasonable, according to the sort of crime in question.

DEFINITION **Bail** is money given to the court that will secure the return of a prisoner who is being temporarily released. Maybe you've heard it said that someone is "out on bail." This means that they were arrested but have paid a certain sum of money in order to be temporarily released. Bail is refunded if the defendant appears at trial as scheduled.

This is the second rule spelled out by the Eighth Amendment. *A person cannot be made to pay unfair fines for a crime.* The punishment must fit the crime.

The last rule you might be familiar with, "cruel and unusual punishment," is a phrase that is often used in connection with our justice system. *A person cannot be subjected to punishment that is either cruel or unusual.*

This rule makes sure that nobody who is convicted of a crime is tortured or dismembered. The Founders just wanted punishments to be within reason.

Of course this, too, is a controversial topic. There have been many debates about what exactly constitutes cruel and unusual punishment.

PRACTICE 1

For each of the following rights, write the number of the corresponding amendment on the line provided.

1. face witnesses against you __________
2. no cruel and unusual punishment __________
3. public trial __________
4. jury trial in civil cases involving more than $20 __________
5. have a lawyer __________
6. find witnesses in favor of your case __________
7. speedy trial __________
8. fair bail __________
9. informed about accusations __________
10. fair jury __________

ANSWERS

1. Sixth
2. Eighth
3. Sixth
4. Seventh
5. Sixth
6. Sixth
7. Sixth
8. Eighth
9. Sixth
10. Sixth

LESSON 13

the ninth and tenth amendments

You can not possibly have a broader basis for any government then that which includes all the people, with all their rights in their hands, and with an equal power to maintain their rights.

—William Lloyd Garrison

This lesson discusses the last two amendments of the Bill of Rights, the Ninth and Tenth Amendments to the Constitution. It explains the amendments by uncovering the meanings of some of the complicated words used by the Founders and talks about the relevance of the two amendments.

NOW WE'VE COME to the last two amendments of the Bill of Rights. Up until this point, the amendments have been fairly specific about rights to which the citizens of the United States are entitled. There have been rights related to life, liberty, and property, including rights of persons accused of a crime. The Ninth and Tenth Amendments fill in any gaps in the description of citizens' rights. It's almost as if the Founders were trying to cover their bases.

NINTH AMENDMENT

Here is the Ninth Amendment written out, with some annotations to explain the wording.

> *The enumeration* (listing) *in the Constitution of certain rights, shall not be construed* (understood) *to deny or disparage* (degrade) *others retained by the people.*

Essentially, this amendment says that although all of these rights are being spelled out in the Constitution there are other rights that are equally significant. Perhaps the Founders figured, We must be leaving *something* out. They knew that there was no way they could possibly list all the rights of citizens of the United States. That's why they wrote the Ninth Amendment, stating that these are not the only rights we have.

ACTIVITY Do you think the Founders left anything out? What might you include if you were creating a Bill of Rights? Take a minute to write some amendments that you would have included.

TENTH AMENDMENT

The Tenth Amendment, the last amendment of the Bill of Rights also ties up any loose ends that might exist in the Constitution. This is what it says.

> *The powers not delegated to the United States by the Constitution, nor prohibited by it to the States, are reserved to the States respectively, or to the people.*

Here, the Founding Fathers are saying that any leftover power lies with the states or the people, NOT with the federal government.

Does it seem strange to you that the Founding Fathers spent a whole amendment on this one point? Well, go back to when we discussed the origin of the Constitution. Remember how the colonists were concerned about the federal government's having too much power? If you think about the struggle the colonists had just been through with the British government, when many felt that they didn't have enough control over their own individual lives, then it makes sense that the words of the Tenth Amendment hold so much importance.

ACTIVITY The first ten amendments to the Constitution, which are the Bill of Rights, don't appear to be written in order of importance. How would you rank them? In your opinion, list the number of each amendment (1–10) in order from most important to least important.

PRACTICE 1

Decide whether each of the following statements is *true* or *false*.

1. The Ninth Amendment filled in any gaps there might have been in the Bill of Rights.
2. If it's not in the Constitution, it's not a right.
3. The Tenth Amendment was added two years after the Ninth Amendment.
4. The Ninth and Tenth Amendments are the least important amendments in the Bill of Rights.
5. The Tenth Amendment is the last amendment to the Bill of Rights.
6. James Madison believed that the amendment wording should be understood in its historical background.
7. Just because a right is not in the Bill of Rights does not mean that it is not a citizen's right.
8. Any power not given to the federal government or denied to the states remains with the states or with the people.
9. The Founding Fathers were concerned that the federal government would have too much power.
10. The Founding Fathers felt they had included everything in the Bill of Rights.

ANSWERS

1. **true**
2. **false.** The Ninth Amendment says that just because the right is not written in the Constitution does not mean it is not a right.
3. **false.** The Tenth Amendment was written at the same time as all the other nine amendments in the Bill of Rights.

4. **false.** Just because they are at the end and are short amendments, does not make the Ninth and Tenth Amendments the least important of the Bill of Rights.
5. **true**
6. **true**
7. **true**
8. **true**
9. **true**
10. **false.** The reason the Founding Fathers included the Ninth Amendment was because they felt it was very possible that they had left something out.

SECTION 4

the eleventh through twenty-third amendments

LESSON 14

the eleventh and twelfth amendments

To seek out the best through the whole Union, we must resort to the information which from the best of men, acting disinterestedly and with the purest motives, is sometimes incorrect.

—THOMAS JEFFERSON

This lesson briefly discusses some of the differences between the previous ten amendments and the amendments to come. You will learn the new rules that were established by the ratifications of the Eleventh and Twelfth Amendments.

UP TO THIS POINT everything we've discussed in this book was written by the Founders either in the original Articles of the Constitution or in the first ten Amendments, which were added shortly after ratification. Now we're entering different territory. The Eleventh through Twenty-Seventh Amendments were added onto the Constitution at various times between the years 1798 and 1992. As you know, the first 10 amendments were included in order to make sure that certain rights were secured for the citizens of the United States. These next 16 amendments have a slightly different purpose. Some are similar in that they also serve to secure the rights of certain groups, but other amendments were each added in order to clarify or fix some problem with the original Constitution and Bill of Rights.

It's only natural that after a document like the Constitution has been written and put into effect, problems arise. Have you ever tried on a pair of shoes in the store and they have seemed really comfortable, but when you got them home and started wearing them around, they started to hurt your feet? Well, this is a similar situation. Sometimes, you have to start using a thing before you know exactly what's wrong with it or how it could be improved. The following lessons discuss how the rest of the Constitution's amendments attempt to solve some problems that arose.

ACTIVITY Think of a time when you had to use something in order to figure out some of its flaws. Take a minute to write a paragraph about what you learned.

ELEVENTH AMENDMENT

Added to the Constitution in 1798, the Eleventh Amendment clarifies the extent of power that belongs to the federal court system of the United States. It explains that the federal judicial (court) system will not deal with cases that are brought against a state by either a citizen of a different state or of another country. To make this clearer, here are some examples.

Joe is a citizen of Virginia and wants to bring a case to a federal court against the state of New York. This is not constitutional. Jennifer is a citizen of France and wants to bring a case to a United States federal court against the state of Maine. The federal court system will not deal with this case, either. The Eleventh Amendment makes clear that the power of the United States judicial system does not extend to cases against one of the states by citizens of other states or other countries.

TWELFTH AMENDMENT

You might remember learning that before the ratification of the Twelfth Amendment, the person who received the second most votes for president became the vice president. But there were problems with this system. In the presidential election of 1800, John Adams was running against Thomas Jefferson. Aaron Burr was, unofficially, Jefferson's vice presidential running mate. Each elector got two votes. Everyone who voted for Jefferson also voted for Burr, giving them the same number of votes and leaving the decision in the hands of Congress.

FUN FACT Vice President Aaron Burr killed Alexander Hamilton in a duel in New Jersey in 1804.

In 1804, the Twelfth Amendment was ratified to clear up the confusion about the presidential election process. According to the Twelfth Amendment, here is how the president and vice president were elected.

Step 1

Within each state, all the electors get together. (Remember that the number of electors in each state is equal to the number of Senators that state has (two), plus the number of Representatives (depends on population).)

Step 2

Each elector casts a vote for president and, on a separate ballot, casts a vote for vice president. At least one of the candidates must not be a resident of the electors' state.

Step 3

The electors make two lists from the information on their ballots. They make one list of all the people who were voted for to fill the position of president and another list of all the people who were voted for to fill the position of vice president. Also, the electors must record the number of votes that each candidate received.

Step 4

Next, the electors sign and certify the lists, then seal them and send them to the president of the Senate.

Step 5

Last, the president of the Senate, in the presence of both the Senate and the House of Representatives, opens all the lists and counts the votes.

Thus, the person who got the most votes for president becomes the president, but only if that person received more than half, or a majority, of the total votes cast for president. If nobody receives more than half of the votes for president, then the House of Representatives chooses the president from among the top three vote getters. In this scenario, each state gets one vote regardless of how many representatives it has, and two-thirds of the states must vote. The person chosen to be president must, again, get a majority of the votes cast by the states.

How the Vice President Is Chosen

This process is supposed to be completed before the president takes office, but if the House of Representatives can't do it by then, the vice president acts as president in the meantime. Maybe you're familiar with the date that the president takes office. Now it is January 20, but it only became January 20 when the Twentieth Amendment was added to the Constitution. According to the Twelfth Amendment, the president takes office on March 4.

Regarding choosing the vice president, the process is basically the same. The vice president also must receive a majority of the electoral votes cast for vice president, but if nobody gets a majority, then the Senate votes instead of the House of Representatives. The Senate chooses from the top two vote getters, and the rest of the voting is the same as for the president. Two-thirds of the Senate must be present for the vote, and the winner must get a majority of the votes.

The Twelfth Amendment also makes clear that if a person is not qualified to be the president, he cannot run for vice president. If you think about it, this makes sense. If something happens to the president that makes him unable to perform his job, it is the vice president who takes over, so he or she needs to be just as qualified as the president.

The Electoral College System

This system has been controversial. Today, citizens go to the polls to vote for president and vice president and, although the electors from that state have pledged to vote for a particular candidate, they are not held to that decision by federal law. Some are held to it by state law. Most states currently have a system whereby all of the state's electors vote for whoever gets the majority of the citizens' votes in that state. This is slightly different from what is described in the Twelfth Amendment, but it still follows the rule, keeping it from being unconstitutional.

PRACTICE 1

Fill in the blanks of the following sentences with one of the words or phrases that follow.

1800	March 4
1804	judicial
president	majority
vice president	House of Representatives
two	Senate

1. The Twelfth Amendment was ratified in ____________.

2. The Eleventh Amendment clarifies what sort of cases the federal ____________ system will handle.

3. Before the Twelfth Amendment was added to the Constitution, the person who received the second most votes in the presidential election became the ____________.

4. According to the Twelfth Amendment, each elector will cast ____________ votes.

5. If a person is not qualified to be ____________, then he cannot be vice president.

6. The person who becomes president must receive a ____________ of the total electoral votes cast for president.

7. If nobody receives more than half the votes, the ____________ chooses from among the top three vote getters.

8. The Twelfth Amendment declares that the president will take office on ____________.

9. If nobody receives a majority of the votes for vice president, the ____________ chooses from among the top two vote getters.

10. In the presidential election of ____________, John Adams ran against Thomas Jefferson.

ANSWERS

1. 1804
2. judicial
3. vice president
4. two
5. president
6. majority
7. House of Representatives
8. March 4
9. Senate
10. 1800

LESSON 15

the thirteenth amendment

A long habit of not thinking a thing wrong gives it a superficial appearance of being right.
—THOMAS PAINE

This lesson teaches you not only about the nuts and bolts of the Thirteenth Amendment, but also about why the ratification of this particular amendment was so important in our country's history.

NOW WE'VE COME to an important amendment in the history of the United States. The Thirteenth Amendment was added in 1865 and makes slavery unconstitutional. Here is section 1 of the amendment.

> *Neither slavery nor involuntary servitude, except as a punishment for crime whereof the party shall have been duly convicted, shall exist within the United States, or any place subject to their jurisdiction.*

As you can see, it's stated fairly plainly. Slavery is not allowed in the United States or in any territory that's ruled by the United States.

DEFINITION **Involuntary servitude** is forced labor.

Maybe you're wondering about the exception. The amendment states that the only exception to the no-slavery rule is as punishment for a crime. If a person is convicted of a crime and sent to prison, they can be forced to do certain jobs while they are there.

Section 2 of the Thirteenth Amendment simply states that

Congress shall have power to enforce this article by appropriate legislation.

In other words, Congress can make laws in order to enforce the no-slavery rule.

FUN FACT At the time the Thirteenth Amendment was ratified, there had not been an amendment added to the Constitution for 61 years.

HISTORICAL CONTEXT

We've established that the Thirteenth Amendment put an end to slavery in the United States, but why was it such an important moment in our country's history? Well, back when the Founders were debating the Constitution, the issue of slavery came up. One big issue was how slaves would count toward a state's representation in the House of Representatives (and thus in the Electoral College as well). Southern states (which had more slaves) wanted slaves to count more toward representation, therefore giving those states greater power in the government. Northern states (which had fewer slaves) wanted the opposite. Remember the three-fifths clause. That was the compromise. Slaves, who were considered property, would count as three-fifths of a person for the purposes of representation.

There were some people from the beginning who were opposed to slavery on moral grounds, and between the ratification of the Constitution in 1787 and the Civil War in 1861, Northern states gradually emancipated their slaves. The issue really came to a head, though, when the United States began to expand west. New states were being added to the Union. The question became, Would the new states be slave states or non-slave states? The answer would have consequences affecting the balance of power in Congress. By the time the Civil War started, the line was distinct. Northern states did not have slaves and Southern states did (even though some of the border states with slaves had sided with the North).

DEFINITIONS **Abolitionist** someone who fought to abolish slavery
Emancipation the act of freeing slaves

Pressure from abolitionists steadily grew and in 1865, the South having lost the Civil War, President Abraham Lincoln helped push the Thirteenth Amendment through to ratification. Abraham Lincoln was our country's sixteenth President. He was assassinated by John Wilkes Booth while attending a play in 1865.

PRACTICE 1

Choose the best answer to each of the following questions.

1. What does the Thirteenth Amendment abolish?
a. cruel and unusual punishment
b. slavery
c. poll tax
d. Senate term limits

2. When was the Thirteenth Amendment ratified?
a. 1863
b. 1864
c. 1865
d. 1866

3. What is the one EXCEPTION to the rule that there will NOT be forced labor?
a. in the case of someone having been convicted of a crime
b. in the case of someone being black
c. in the case of someone being poor
d. in the case of someone being an immigrant

4. According to the Thirteenth Amendment, is slavery allowed in territories controlled by the United States?
a. yes
b. no
c. only in certain territories
d. The Thirteenth Amendment does not say.

5. In the original Constitutional debate, which states wanted slaves to count toward representation in the federal government?
a. all of the states
b. Northern states
c. Southern states
d. none of the states

6. What was one of the main issues that brought slavery to the forefront of political debate in the early 1860s?
a. sanitation policy
b. immigration policy
c. westward expansion
d. none of the above

7. Who pushed the Thirteenth Amendment through to ratification?
a. Abraham Lincoln
b. Andrew Jackson
c. George Washington
d. John Quincy Adams

8. Why was the ratification of the Thirteenth Amendment such an important moment in our country's history?
a. because the institution of slavery had been a fixture in the country for a long time
b. because the debate about slavery rested heavily on the issue of political power in Congress
c. because some people believed that slavery was morally wrong
d. all of the above

9. What is *involuntary servitude*?
a. deportation
b. forced labor
c. political status
d. a state of mind

10. Who won the Civil War?
a. Northern and border states that had remained in the Union
b. Southern states that had broken away from the Union
c. it was a tie
d. new Western states that had just been added to the Union

ANSWERS

1. **b.** The Thirteenth Amendment abolished slavery in the United States and its territories.
2. **c.** The Thirteenth Amendment was ratified in 1865.
3. **a.** According to the Thirteenth Amendment, forced labor is allowed if a person has been convicted of a crime.
4. **b.** No, according to the Thirteenth Amendment, slavery is NOT allowed in any territory controlled by the United States.
5. **c.** Southern states wanted slaves to count toward representation in the federal government because, since they had more slaves, they would have more power in Congress.
6. **c.** The issue of slavery came to the forefront of debate when territories in the west applied for statehood. Would those states be slave states or non-slave states?
7. **a.** Abraham Lincoln pushed the Thirteenth Amendment through to ratification.
8. **d.** The answer is *all of the above*. Slavery had been an institution for a long time in this country, the issue rested on political power in Congress, and some people were morally against it.
9. **b.** *Involuntary servitude* is forced labor.
10. **a.** The Northern and border states that had remained in the Union won the Civil War.

LESSON 16

the fourteenth amendment

If there is no struggle, there is no progress.
—Frederick Douglass

This lesson discusses some consequences of the end of the Civil War. You will learn how the Fourteenth Amendment establishes the definition of a citizen and assigns a punishment for those who had fought for the South during the war.

BACKGROUND

Added to the Constitution in 1868, the Fourteenth Amendment defines what makes a person a citizen of the United States and how some people who had fought against the Union would be punished. The South had lost and slavery was abolished, but then there were the questions of who was a citizen, what rights blacks had in the South, and whether there would be a punishment for those who had left the Union. The Fourteenth Amendment answers these questions.

Section 1

Section 1 of the Fourteenth Amendment defines who is a citizen of the United States. There are two ways a person can be a citizen. You can either be born in the United States, which automatically makes you a citizen, or you can be made a citizen after birth. To be made a citizen legally, after birth, is called being **naturalized**.

All citizens of the United States are ruled by the government and are not only citizens of the country, but also of the state in which they live. You might remember that the Fifth Amendment spells out some rules that the federal government has to follow regarding citizens. The Fourteenth Amendment extends those rules to the states. It says that states are not allowed to make laws that restrict people's rights as U.S. citizens and cannot deprive citizens of life, liberty, or property without due process of law. They also cannot keep a person from receiving equal treatment under the law.

Section 2

Do you remember how in the original text of the Constitution slaves were counted as three-fifths of person for the purposes of representation in Congress? Well, now slavery had been abolished. Section 2 of the Fourteenth Amendment declares that the number of representatives a state has in Congress is dependent on the total number of people in that state. Former slaves were now counted as whole people.

This section also makes clear that if a person is male and is older than 21 years of age, he should be allowed to vote. To encourage states to allow former slaves to vote, the writers of the Fourteenth Amendment threatened that a state would lose representatives in Congress proportional to the number of people who were qualified to vote in the state, but were kept from doing so. Any state that barred former slaves from voting would, consequently, have fewer representatives in Congress.

ACTIVITY Do you think that decreased representation is an effective punishment? Why or why not?

Section 3

This section of the Fourteenth Amendment lays down a punishment for those who defected from the Union during the Civil War. It states that a person cannot be a Senator, Representative, elector, civil officer, or military officer in the United States or any state if he had taken an oath to support the Constitution and then engaged in "insurrection or rebellion against" the United States "or [gave] aid or comfort to the enemies thereof." Basically, a person was not allowed to work as a government official if before the Civil War they had been sworn in as a government official and had then became a Confederate.

DEFINITION Confederate a person who supported the Confederacy, which was the government formed when the Southern states seceded from the Union during the Civil War.

This was the punishment for those in the government who had fought against the Union in the war. However, the amendment also states that if two-thirds of both houses of Congress vote to do so, the punishment can be reversed. So the authors of this particular amendment inevitably left it to Congress to decide if the punishment should stick. (In the end, President Andrew Johnson pardoned thousands of former Confederates, so this provision did have little effect.)

Section 4

After the Civil War ended there was some question as to what would happen to debts that had been accumulated while soldiers were fighting the war. Section 4 of the Fourteenth Amendment says that any debts that were created by the United States in its attempt to end the Civil War will be paid. However, any debts created by the Southern States will not be paid. They will be invalid and states will not be allowed either to accept payment or to give payment for these debts. Also mentioned in this section of the amendment is the fact that nobody would be compensated for the loss of slaves who were set free.

Section 5

Like Section 4 of the previous amendment, Section 5 of the Fourteenth Amendment states that Congress has the power to make laws that support this amendment, allowing it to work. This provision clarified that it was not for the courts and the state governments alone, but primarily for the Congress, to enforce this amendment.

PRACTICE 1

Decide whether the following statements are *true* or *false*.

1. The Fourteenth Amendment was added to the Constitution in 1865.

2. There are two ways that a person can be a citizen of the United States.

3. If you were born in the United States, then you are automatically a citizen.

4. You cannot legally become a citizen if you were not born in the United States.

5. If you are a citizen of the United States, you are also a citizen of the state in which you live.

6. After the Fourteenth Amendment had been ratified, former slaves still counted as three-fifths of a person for the purposes of representation in the federal government.

7. According to the Fourteenth Amendment, if you were a male citizen of the United States and at least twenty-one years old, you were qualified to vote.

8. States are not allowed to keep qualified people from voting.

9. A government official who had become a Confederate during the Civil War was still allowed to work in the government.

10. Nobody would be compensated for the loss of slaves during the Civil War.

11. Congress has the power to overturn the punishment issued by the Fourteenth Amendment to people who had become Confederates during the Civil War.

12. States are allowed to restrict people's rights as citizens of the United States.

ANSWERS

1. **false.** The Fourteenth Amendment was added to the Constitution in 1868.
2. **true.**
3. **true.**
4. **false.** You can legally become a citizen of the United States, even if you were not born in the country.
5. **true.**
6. **false.** According to the Fourteenth Amendment, representation will be based on the *total* number of people residing in each state.
7. **true.**
8. **false.** This is a tricky one. According to the Fourteenth Amendment, states are, in fact, allowed to keep qualified people from voting, BUT if they do, they will be punished by receiving fewer representatives in Congress.
9. **false.** The Fourteenth Amendment makes it clear that any government official who became a Confederate during the Civil War would not be allowed to work for the government again.
10. **true.**
11. **true.**
12. **false.** States are NOT allowed to restrict people's rights as citizens of the United States.

LESSON 17

the fifteenth amendment

One great object of the Constitution was to restrain majorities from oppressing minorities or encroaching upon just rights.
—James K. Polk

This lesson explains the rights that were secured by the ratification of the Fifteenth Amendment and how those rights are relevant today.

YOU PROBABLY REMEMBER learning about how the Fourteenth Amendment attempted to encourage states to allow former slaves to vote, by decreasing their number of representatives in Congress if they kept qualified people from voting. Well, two years after the Fourteenth Amendment had been ratified, Congress ratified the Fifteenth Amendment in 1870, making it clear that former slaves would be allowed to vote.

This is the text of Section 1 of the Fifteenth Amendment.

The right of citizens of the United States to vote shall not be denied or abridged by the United States or by any State on account of race, color, or previous condition of servitude.

As you can see, it says fairly clearly that the right of a person to vote cannot be denied based on "race, color, or previous condition of servitude." You can also see that the authors of this amendment were covering their bases. They don't just say that the right to vote cannot be denied on account of "previous condition of servitude," which directly refers to former slaves. They also include "race" and "color." So, this generality makes it difficult for a state to get around the amendment.

In the Fourteenth Amendment they had made a mistake. They had not made it clear enough that former slaves would be allowed to vote. Even though they had created a situation that made it undesirable for a state to keep former slaves from voting, they had not made it unconstitutional. States were still keeping former slaves from voting. The Fifteenth Amendment made denying former slaves the right to vote unconstitutional.

ACTIVITY Think about some ways in which the kids at your school don't have equal rights. Are some people allowed to do things that others aren't? If you discover any, and if you think this is wrong, write a letter to your principal explaining why you think it is wrong.

Section 2 of the Fifteenth Amendment states that Congress has the power to make laws in order to enforce the amendment.

Think about all the kids in your school and in your community. Imagine if all the kids who have darker skin or are of other races were not allowed to do the same things that the white kids were. Imagine if when those kids got old enough to vote, they weren't allowed to do so. They would not be privileged to have the same rights as other citizens and would not be represented in the government. The ratification of this amendment leveled the playing field. It paved the way for future generations to have equal rights and to have their voices heard.

PRACTICE 1

Circle the word or phrase that best fits the sentence.

1. The Fifteenth Amendment was ratified in (1871/1870).
2. The (Fourteenth/Fifteenth) Amendment encouraged states to let all qualified people vote.
3. According to the Fourteenth Amendment, if a state prevented qualified people from voting, their number of representatives in Congress would be (increased/decreased).

4. The ratification of the Fifteenth Amendment was a way to (erase/fix) the Fourteenth Amendment.

5. The Fifteenth Amendment states that a person (cannot/can) be denied the right to vote based on "race, color, or previous condition of servitude."

6. "Previous condition of servitude" refers directly to (former Congressmen/former slaves).

7. Section 2 of the Fifteenth Amendment says that Congress has the power to make (money/laws) in order to enforce the amendment.

8. The right to (vote/own property) is important, because it gives a person the chance to choose who will represent them in Congress.

9. The Fifteenth Amendment says that a person cannot be denied the right to vote based on the color of their (eyes/skin).

10. The phrasing of the Fifteenth Amendment is purposely general in order to (include everyone; exclude everyone).

ANSWERS

1. **1870**
2. **fourteenth**
3. **decreased**
4. **fix**
5. **cannot**
6. **former slaves**
7. **laws**
8. **vote**
9. **skin**
10. **include**

LESSON 18

the sixteenth and seventeenth amendments

Our Constitution is in actual operation; everything appears to promise that it will last; but in this world nothing is certain but death and taxes.

—Benjamin Franklin

This lesson explains the changes in rules that both the Sixteenth and Seventeenth Amendments created. You will learn how the Sixteenth Amendment alters how Congress collects taxes and how the Seventeenth Amendment alters how Senators are elected.

THE SIXTEENTH AND SEVENTEENTH Amendments were ratified in the same year, 1913. Both reflect the Progressive Movement's goal of centralizing America's government: of giving the Federal government more power. One has to do with taxes and the other with the election of Senators. Let's begin by taking a look at the Sixteenth Amendment, the one about taxes.

SIXTEENTH AMENDMENT

If you remember, Section 9 of Article I of the Constitution says that each state will pay taxes to the federal government in proportion to the number of people who live in that state. Well, the Sixteenth Amendment changes this rule. This is the text of the amendment.

The Congress shall have power to lay and collect taxes on incomes, from whatever source derived, without apportionment among the several States, and without regard to any census or enumeration.

Looking more closely at the second half of the amendment first, you can see that it refers to the old rule.

without apportionment among the several States, and without regard to any census or enumeration.

DEFINITION Enumeration the counting of something.

What this second half says is that Congress does not have to collect taxes based on how many people live in a particular state. This allows Congress to be less restricted in how much it can collect in taxes. While the second half of the amendment talks about the lifting of this restriction, the first half mentions what the Congress will now have the power to do.

to lay and collect taxes on incomes, from whatever source derived.

This means that Congress is now allowed to collect taxes from peoples' incomes. Notice that the amendment specifically states "from whatever source derived." It doesn't matter how a person acquired their money. They could be a farmer, a banker, a lawyer, or a dentist. It's all the same to Congress. Starting in 1913, with the ratification of this amendment, Congress has the power to tax anyone's income, regardless of how they make their living.

SEVENTEENTH AMENDMENT

Nineteen-thirteen was a big year for amendments. Two in one year! But, unlike the Sixteenth Amendment, which deals with Congress taxing income, the Seventeenth Amendment deals with how Senators are elected. The amendments have one similarity, however. Both serve to alter a rule that was laid out in Article I of the original text of the Constitution.

Section 3 of Article I states that each state's legislature would elect the two senators that would represent that state in Congress. You might remember that this was a way for the Founders to ensure that only qualified people be elected to the Senate. They didn't trust the ordinary citizen to choose someone for such an important position. In addition, it gave state legislatures a way to keep Congress from grabbing the states' reserved powers. But in 1913, the ratification of the Seventeenth Amendment changed all that.

The Seventeenth Amendment repeats that there will be two Senators from each state and that each Senator will serve a six-year term. In Congress, each senator will get one vote. The difference is that, starting with the ratification of this amendment, senators will be elected directly by the people. Citizens will go to the polls and vote for who they want their Senators to be.

ACTIVITY Do you think the direct election of Senators is better than having the state legislatures choose? Why or why not?

Maybe you're wondering why Congress decided to make the switch from Senators elected by state legislatures to Senators elected directly by the people. Well, it turns out that the process wasn't working very well. Some state legislatures were having a difficult time deciding who to elect due to disagreements between political parties. In some cases, Senate seats would be vacant for years because of the disagreements. Also, having citizens choose Senators directly gave them more power in the government. People started lobbying for direct election and in 1913 the amendment went through.

Also described in the Seventeenth Amendment is what will happen if there is a vacancy in the Senate. First, the governor of the state will call for a special election. Then, the state legislature will be in charge of the election and has the authority to allow the governor to choose an acting senator until the election can be held.

PRACTICE 1

Decide whether each of the following phrases refers to the Sixteenth Amendment, to the Seventeenth Amendment, or to both. Place the number of the question under each amendment.

Sixteenth Amendment	Seventeenth Amendment

1. Ratified in 1913
2. If there is a vacancy in the Senate, the governor will call for a special election.
3. Deals with the election of Senators
4. Senators will be elected directly by the people.
5. Deals with taxes
6. Alters a rule from the original text of the Constitution
7. Congress does not have to collect taxes based on the population of the state.
8. Prior to this amendment, some Senate seats had been vacant for years.
9. Congress can collect taxes from incomes.
10. State legislatures will no longer choose Senators.

ANSWERS

Sixteenth Amendment	Seventeenth Amendment
1, 5, 6, 7, 9	1, 2, 3, 4, 6, 8, 10

LESSON 19

the eighteenth and twenty-first amendments

It is the genius of our Constitution that under its shelter of enduring institutions and rooted principles there is ample room for the rich fertility of American political invention.

—LYNDON B. JOHNSON

This lesson discusses the Eighteenth Amendment and the Twenty-first Amendment, which repealed the Eighteenth. You will learn about Prohibition and what the country was like during the time between the two amendments. Also, you will discover the intention behind the amendments.

YOU MIGHT BE wondering why this lesson skips the Nineteenth and Twentieth Amendments. Well, as you'll see, the Eighteenth and Twenty-first Amendments are very closely related. In fact, the whole point of the Twenty-first Amendment is to repeal, or take back, the Eighteenth Amendment. Here's the beginning of the story. It starts with the Eighteenth Amendment.

DEFINITION **Repeal** to officially take back or undo.

EIGHTEENTH AMENDMENT

In 1919 the Eighteenth Amendment to the Constitution was ratified by Congress. The amendment put into effect something called **Prohibition**. You may have heard the term before. Prohibition refers to a period of time in the United States when the manufacture, sale, and transport of alcohol was not allowed. This is what Section 1 of the Eighteenth Amendment says.

> *After one year from the ratification of this article the manufacture, sale, or transportation of intoxicating liquors within, the importation thereof into, or the exportation thereof from the United States and all territory subject to the jurisdiction thereof for beverage purposes is hereby prohibited.*

The first phrase declares when the prohibition of alcohol will take effect.

> *After one year from the ratification of this article*

So Prohibition began exactly one year after the Eighteenth Amendment had been ratified. Next, the Amendment describes what specifically will not be allowed.

> *the manufacture, sale, or transportation of intoxicating liquors*

Not only were you not allowed to sell alcohol, or "intoxicating liquors," but you could not even manufacture it. You also could not transport it within the United States, to the United States, from the United States, or within, to, or from any territory controlled by the United States. Essentially, there was to be no business or trade involving alcohol. It was to be done away with entirely.

But why did lawmakers in 1919 want to do away with alcohol? For years, decades even, there had been people who believed that banning alcohol would create a more moral society and lead to greater progress and the achievement of personal goals. They blamed alcohol for many of the problems they saw in society. This belief gained support and in 1919 there were enough supporters to get the amendment ratified.

FUN FACT Prohibition was also known as *The Noble Experiment*.

THE UNITED STATES DURING PROHIBITION

Now, it's one year after the ratification of the Eighteenth Amendment and manufacturing, selling, and transportation of alcohol is officially outlawed. As you might imagine, this had a large effect on the country. Lots of money was spent attempting to enforce the new rule, but law enforcers had a difficult time. First, the amendment itself had a loophole. You could not manufacture alcohol, but it didn't say you couldn't drink it. And, since the amendment did not take effect until one year after it had been ratified, people stocked up on legally bought alcohol and just drank that during Prohibition.

Second, now that the alcohol industry had been shut down, a whole new industry sprang up, the underground alcohol industry. People began manufacturing and selling alcohol illegally. Some began to frequent secret establishments, called speakeasies, in order to drink alcohol. So, what began as an attempt to create a more moral society, simply added more corruption.

DEFINITION During Prohibition, Al Capone, a gangster from Chicago, made lots of money from bootlegging. *Bootlegging* is the act of making and selling alcohol illegally.

TWENTY-FIRST AMENDMENT

Fourteen years after the Eighteenth Amendment had been ratified, it was repealed by the ratification of the Twenty-first Amendment, thereby ending Prohibition. Section 1 of the Twenty-first Amendment simply states that:

> *The eighteenth article of amendment to the Constitution of the United States is hereby repealed.*

DEFINITION **Repeal** to take back or undo.

The Eighteenth Amendment was the only amendment ever to be repealed by another amendment.

So you see, the Eighteenth Amendment was passed with the intention of creating a more moral society, prohibiting the manufacture and sale of alcoholic beverages. But people found ways of getting around it and simply moved everything into a more hidden realm. Fourteen years later, it was clear that Prohibition wasn't working out and the Twenty-first Amendment was ratified, repealing the Eighteenth Amendment.

PRACTICE 1

Choose the best answer to each of the following questions.

1. Which amendment does the Twenty-first Amendment repeal?
- **a.** 17
- **b.** 18
- **c.** 19
- **d.** 20

2. What does the Eighteenth Amendment ban the manufacture of?
- **a.** cigarettes
- **b.** guns
- **c.** alcohol
- **d.** candy

3. The period of time during which the Eighteenth Amendment was in effect is often referred to as what?
- **a.** The Golden Age
- **b.** Indiscretion
- **c.** Prohibition
- **d.** The Era

4. What three things does the Eighteenth Amendment specify you are NOT allowed to do with alcohol?
- **a.** manufacture it, sell it, and transport it
- **b.** sell it, manufacture it, and drink it
- **c.** buy it, manufacture it, and drink it
- **d.** import it, drink it, and manufacture it

5. The Eighteenth Amendment was ratified in what year?
   a. 1919
   b. 1920
   c. 1921
   d. 1922

6. In which year did the Eighteenth Amendment's ban on alcohol take effect?
   a. 1919
   b. 1920
   c. 1921
   d. 1922

7. Why did lawmakers pass the Eighteenth Amendment?
   a. Many people believed that alcohol was the source of many of society's problems.
   b. They were pressured by the citizens of France.
   c. They wanted to be able to ratify the Twenty-first Amendment.
   d. They were bored.

8. For how many years did Prohibition last?
   a. 10
   b. 12
   c. 14
   d. 16

9. What did people do during Prohibition?
   a. manufactured alcohol illegally
   b. drank alcohol that they had purchased legally before the ban had taken effect
   c. patronized secret establishments that served alcohol illegally, known as speakeasies
   d. all of the above

10. Why was the Twenty-first Amendment, repealing the ban on alcohol, ratified?

- **a.** pressure from speakeasy owners
- **b.** Congress wanted to host a cocktail party.
- **c.** The Twentieth Amendment didn't work.
- **d.** Prohibition did not accomplish what its supporters had intended it to accomplish.

ANSWERS

1. **b.** The Twenty-first Amendment repeals the Eighteenth Amendment.
2. **c.** The Eighteenth Amendment bans the manufacture of alcohol.
3. **c.** The period of time in which the Eighteenth Amendment was in effect is often referred to as Prohibition.
4. **a.** The Eighteenth Amendment states that you cannot manufacture, sell, or transport alcohol.
5. **a.** The Eighteenth Amendment was ratified in 1919.
6. **b.** The ban on alcohol did not take effect until 1920, one year after the amendment's ratification.
7. **a.** Some people blamed alcohol for society's problems.
8. **c.** Prohibition lasted for 14 years.
9. **d.** During Prohibition people manufactured alcohol illegally, drank alcohol that they had purchased legally before the ban had taken effect, and went to speakeasies.
10. **d.** The Eighteenth Amendment was repealed by the Twenty-first Amendment because Prohibition had not accomplished what its supporters had hoped.

LESSON 20

the nineteenth amendment

There never will be complete equality until women themselves help to make laws and elect lawmakers.

—Susan B. Anthony

This lesson takes a look at the Women's Suffrage Movement in the United States. You will learn about the Nineteenth Amendment and the impact it had on women in this country.

ONE HUNDRED THIRTY-THREE years elapsed between the drafting of the original Constitution and the ratification of the Nineteenth Amendment. That's more than six generations. Try to think back six generations in your family. You might not even know your family tree that far back. Needless to say, a lot of time passed between when those Founders had debated the Constitution in that stuffy room in Philadelphia and when the Nineteenth Amendment made its mark on the citizens of the United States.

The Nineteenth Amendment was an important moment in our history. It is the amendment that secured the right for women to vote. For 134 years, women had been citizens of the United States, abiding by all the same rules and regulations as all the other citizens, but although they had voted in some states, they had not had a federal right to vote. But why not? Perhaps it seems silly today. Of course women should be allowed to vote. For over 90 years, women have had the same constitutional rights as men, so it can be difficult to imagine so different a situation.

ACTIVITY Imagine that the students in your school were put in charge of voting for a new principal. Now imagine that only the boys are allowed to vote. How would you feel about this?

In the beginning, women were largely absent from the political process. But as time went on, more and more women desired to have a hand in deciding who would represent them in government. After all, the government was not truly representative of the people unless all the adults had a part in choosing their representatives.

It can be difficult to pinpoint the beginning of something like the Women's Suffrage Movement, but there was one event in 1848 that seemed to set things in motion. A group of abolitionists (mostly women) met that year to discuss the issue of women's rights. They left the meeting with a declaration, that all "men *and women* are created equal." The movement's leaders, like Susan B. Anthony and Elizabeth Cady Stanton, spent decades lobbying for their cause and gathering support. And while it was the notion that women were equal to men that was the movement's original emphasis, it was the exact opposite that led to the ratification of the Nineteenth Amendment.

DEFINITION **Suffrage** the right to vote

In the latter years of the Women's Suffrage Movement, its supporters began emphasizing the differences between men and women and using that as the justification to give women the right to vote. They argued that a woman's domesticity and maternal instincts would be beneficial to the country. This argument served a wide variety of political agendas and eventually led to women obtaining the right to vote.

The text of the Nineteenth Amendment is clear and straightforward.

> *The right of citizens of the United States to vote shall not be denied or abridged by the United States or by any State on account of sex.*

It simply states that neither the federal government nor any state government can deny or limit the right to vote based on the gender of a person.

As you might imagine, the ratification of this amendment had far-reaching consequences. Suddenly, there were nearly double the number of eligible voters. Those running for office had a whole new segment of the population to please. Finally, the voices of millions of women would be heard.

PRACTICE 1

Decide whether the following statements are either *true* or *false.*

1. Women have always had the right to vote.
2. The Nineteenth Amendment was ratified in 1920.
3. The Women's Suffrage Movement was sudden and fleeting.
4. Although some states allowed them to vote, women had no federal right to vote before the ratification of the Nineteenth Amendment.
5. A meeting in 1848 of female abolitionists was part of the beginning of the Women's Suffrage Movement.
6. Susan B. Anthony was a leader of the Women's Suffrage Movement.
7. Elizabeth Cady Stanton was against the Nineteenth Amendment.
8. In the beginning, it was the differences between men and women that were the focus of the issue of equality between the genders.
9. In the end, it was the differences between men and women that helped promote the Nineteenth Amendment.
10. The Nineteenth Amendment secured the right for women to vote in the United States.

ANSWERS

1. **false.** Women did not always have the right to vote. The Nineteenth Amendment changed that by making it unconstitutional to deny a citizen the right to vote based on gender.
2. **true.**
3. **false.** The Women's Suffrage Movement was not sudden or fleeting. It developed over time and took many years to reach one of its goals, securing the right for women to vote.
4. **false.** Women could not vote before the ratification of the Nineteenth Amendment.
5. **true.**
6. **true.**
7. **false.** Elizabeth Cady Stanton was a leader of the Women's Suffrage Movement and was a supporter of the Nineteenth Amendment.
8. **false.** In the beginning, it was what the genders had in common that was the focus of the issue of equality.
9. **true.**
10. **true.**

LESSON 21

the twentieth, twenty-second, and twenty-third amendments

Posterity: you will never know how much it has cost my generation to preserve your freedom. I hope you will make good use of it.

—John Quincy Adams

This lesson explains the contents of the Twentieth, Twenty-second, and Twenty-third Amendments. You will learn how each of these amendments changed something from the original wording of the Constitution and why those changes were made.

EACH OF THE THREE amendments featured in this lesson is either about the offices of the president and vice president or about voting. Again, keep in mind as you make your way through the lesson that each amendment to the Constitution serves to correct or change in some way the original text written by the Founders.

TWENTIETH AMENDMENT

Ratified in 1933, the Twentieth Amendment takes care of some matters related to the offices of president, vice president, and members of Congress. Section 1 begins by explaining that the terms of the president and vice president will end at noon on January 20 and that the terms of both senators and representatives will end at noon on January 3.

One of the things that Article I says is that Congress is to meet at least once a year. Well, Section 2 of the Twentieth Amendment declares specifically that Congress must meet on January 3 each year. Although, in case that's a bad day for everybody, Section 2 also says that Congress can pass a law to change the date of the meeting.

Section 3 states that if the president elect dies before he takes office, then the vice president becomes the president. If, by some set of circumstances, there is no president elect by January 20 at noon, the vice president becomes the *acting* president. Notice the distinction there between *being* president and being the *acting* president. If a person is *acting* president, we presume that the job is temporary and that at some point someone else will take over. So that all loose ends are tied, Section 3 also states that Congress can pass a law to identify who would act as president or how that person should be chosen, if a situation arises in which at noon on January 20 there is no qualified president elect or vice president.

If Congress must decide who becomes president because nobody received a majority of the electoral votes for president *and* one of the candidates dies, Section 4 of the Twentieth Amendment says that it is up to Congress to decide what to do at that time. Section 5 explains that after the Twentieth Amendment is ratified, Sections 1 and 2 will be effective as of October 15. This means that if the Amendment is ratified between October 15 and January 3 (the day when terms end for Congressmen), then the dates described in Sections 1 and 2 will not take effect until the following year.

Section 6 gives the Twentieth Amendment an expiration date. If the amendment is not ratified in seven years, it is no longer legal.

Thus, the Twentieth Amendment shortened the time period between a presidential election and when he was sworn into office. As you might be aware, a new president is elected in November, but doesn't take office until January. This period of time when the previous president is still in charge is commonly referred to as the **lame duck** period. He's still the president, but not for long. Before the Twentieth Amendment was ratified, this period was even longer than it is now and was creating problems by allowing the lame duck president to do all sorts of things before leaving office, even though he was officially on his way out.

TWENTY-SECOND AMENDMENT

The first president of the United States, George Washington, started a tradition for term limits. He served his first term, ran for one more term and then called it quits, even though people loved him and would have liked him to continue as president. Washington thought it wasn't good for the country to have one person in power too long. Until 1940, when Franklin D. Roosevelt ran for and won a third term as president, the tradition was followed. After Roosevelt became president for an unheard of fourth term in office, Congress decided that it needed to institute an official rule for term limits.

Therefore, in 1951 the Twenty-second Amendment prohibited a person from being elected more than twice to the office of president. So, if a person runs for president, wins, then runs for president again and wins, that's it. At the end of their second term, they can no longer be president. It doesn't matter, either, whether the terms are back to back. Even though Grover Cleveland was president before this amendment was ratified, his presidency is an example of serving two non-consecutive terms. He was elected in both 1884 and 1892, with Benjamin Harrison serving a term in between.

What happens when someone ends up serving part of a term, like Calvin Coolidge, who took over as president in 1923 when President Warren G. Harding died in office? The Twenty-second Amendment makes it clear that if a person is either president or acting president for more than two years of a term to which someone else was elected, this counts as one term. That person can then be elected to the office of president only *one* other time.

FUN FACT President William Henry Harrison served the shortest term in office. He died of pneumonia on April 4, 1841, only 31 days after having been sworn in.

In case there was any confusion, the amendment also states that this new rule does not apply until after the president who is in office at the time of ratification is no longer president.

TWENTY-THIRD AMENDMENT

This amendment, ratified in 1961, revolves around the issue of voting in Washington, DC. Washington, DC is an interesting case. As you probably know, it is the capital of the United States and the location of the federal government. But it is not a state. It is a city whose voters do not reside within any of the 50 states that make up our country.

FUN FACT The *DC* in Washington, DC stands for *District of Columbia*. It is called this because the city was built on land that used to be part of Virginia and Maryland. That land was referred to as *The Territory of Columbia*, named after Christopher Columbus.

Since Washington, DC is not a state, the Twenty-third Amendment explains how the number of electors for the city will be chosen when the time comes for voting for president. The amendment says that the number of electors for the nation's capital will be chosen as if it were a state. So, the number of electors will be equal to the number of senators plus the number of representatives it *would* have if it were a state. (Since Washington, DC is not a state, it does not have any senators or representatives in Congress.) However, the number of electors from Washington, DC cannot be greater than the number of electors from the least populous state.

Before the Twenty-third Amendment, residents of Washington, DC could not vote for president. As the population of the city grew, it didn't seem right for the people who lived there not to be allowed to vote for such a major position. It's important to note that the amendment does not make Washington, DC a state, nor does it give representation for its citizens in Congress.

ACTIVITY How would you feel if you lived in Washington, DC and didn't have any representation in Congress?

PRACTICE 1

Decide which amendment the following statements match and circle the correct number.

1. A president can serve only two terms in office. (20, 22, 23)
2. The citizens of our nation's capital can now vote for president. (20, 22, 23)
3. Washington, DC will get the number of electors it would receive if it were a state. (20, 22, 23)
4. A president's term ends at noon on January 20. (20, 22, 23)
5. The number of electors for Washington, DC cannot be greater than the number of electors for the least populous state. (20, 22, 23)
6. George Washington set a tradition for presidential term limits. (20, 22, 23)
7. Franklin D. Roosevelt was elected to the presidency four times. (20, 22, 23)
8. The terms for senators and representatives end at noon on January 3. (20, 22, 23)
9. If there is no president by noon on January 20, then the vice president will become the acting president. (20, 22, 23)
10. If nobody gets a majority of the vote for president and one of the candidates dies, Congress decides what to do. (20, 22, 23)

ANSWERS

1. 22
2. 23
3. 23
4. 20
5. 23
6. 22
7. 22
8. 20
9. 20
10. 20

LESSON 22

the twenty-fourth through twenty-seventh amendments

Every government degenerates when trusted to the rulers of the people alone. The people themselves are its only safe depositories.
—THOMAS JEFFERSON

This lesson introduces you to the last four amendments that were added to the Constitution. You will learn how each one makes its contribution to how our government operates.

THE FOUR AMENDMENTS discussed in this lesson range in topic from voting rights to congressional pay scales. As you've seen throughout this book so far, each amendment makes a small adjustment to the Constitution in order to get a little closer to fairness and clarity.

TWENTY-FOURTH AMENDMENT

You've probably never heard of a poll tax, since in 1964, the Twenty-fourth Amendment made it unconstitutional. A poll tax is a fee that a person had to pay in order to vote. The Twenty-fourth Amendment says that a person cannot be prevented from voting in any election for president, vice president, electors, senators, or representatives just because he or she has not paid a poll tax.

The poll tax was one of the last ways that people tried to keep black people from voting. Basically, since voting required a fee, only the more wealthy, and often white, members of the population would be able to vote. The Twenty-fourth Amendment finally did away with this loophole.

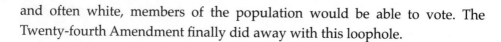

ACTIVITY Do you think there are still loopholes in place that keep certain groups of people from voting? If so, write a letter to your representative in Congress explaining the injustice and how it might be fixed.

TWENTY-FIFTH AMENDMENT

Ever wonder what happens if the president is no longer able to work? What if he gets removed from office? What if something happens to the vice president? The Twenty-fifth Amendment, ratified in 1967, answers these questions and spells out exactly what should be done in certain circumstances.

Section 1 states that if the president is removed from office, dies, or resigns, then the vice president becomes the president. According to Section 2, if, for some reason, there is no vice president, the president will nominate someone for the position. Then, after a majority of each house of Congress confirms the president's choice, that person would become the vice president.

Section 3 of the Twenty-fifth Amendment explains what happens if the president decides he can no longer perform his duties. He must write a letter to the president pro tempore of the Senate and the Speaker of the House, explaining the situation. Then, the vice president becomes the acting president. If the President later feels he can resume his duties, he must write another letter to the president pro tempore of the Senate and the Speaker of the House, saying so. If, as Section 4 explains, the president is sick and cannot perform his duties *or* write his own letters, the vice president is permitted to write and send the letters for him. However, a majority of the president's **cabinet** must agree. (Congress can also choose a group of people other than the president's cabinet to second the vice president's decision to send the letters.)

Now, suppose the president gets better and wants to continue as president. He must again send letters to the president pro tempore of the Senate and the Speaker of the House saying that he would like his job back. If a majority of the president's cabinet (or the other group chosen by Congress) disagrees with the president and believes that he is not able to continue as president, they have four days to make a declaration to Congress regarding the matter. At this time, Congress must meet within 48 hours and has 21 days to decide what to do. If two-thirds of the House of Representatives and two-thirds of the

Senate vote that the president is unable to resume his job, the vice president remains acting president. Otherwise, the president gets back to work.

TWENTY-SIXTH AMENDMENT

According to the Twenty-sixth Amendment, any citizen of the United States who is eighteen years old or older has the right to vote. Ratified in 1971, this is what the Twenty-sixth Amendment made clear. The Fourteenth Amendment had established that a person had to be twenty-one years old in order to vote, but when the Vietnam War started and eighteen-year-olds were being drafted and often dying for their country, Congress decided to change the amendment. If a person was old enough to die for his country, many believed that he was then also old enough to vote for the leader of that country.

FUN FACT Before 1971, each state had its own rule for how old a person had to be to vote. The Twenty-sixth Amendment made the age the same in every state.

TWENTY-SEVENTH AMENDMENT

Originally proposed in 1789 as part of the Bill of Rights, the Twenty-Seventh Amendment was not ratified until 1992, more than two centuries later. Here is the text of the amendment.

> No law, varying the compensation for the services of the Senators and Representatives, shall take effect, until an election of Representatives shall have intervened.

When you think about it, this amendment seems logical. Essentially, what it says is that if Congress makes a law that changes the salaries of congressmen, the salary cannot take effect until the start of the next term. Imagine if this weren't the rule. Congress could make a law that increased its own pay. That doesn't seem right, does it? The Twenty-Seventh Amendment safeguards against greed in Congress by saying that, sure, you can make a law that increases your pay, but it will only affect those people who are elected to the next term in office.

PRACTICE 1

Answer the following questions with a word or phrase.

1. What did the Twenty-Fourth Amendment get rid of? ________________
2. What is a poll tax? ____________________
3. Who becomes president if the president dies or resigns? ______________
4. According to the Twenty-Sixth Amendment, how old do you have to be to vote? ____________________
5. What does the president have to send to the president pro tempore of the Senate and the Speaker of the House in order to get his job back if he has been ill, but is able to work again? ____________________
6. How many days does Congress have to decide whether to let the president resume his duties? ____________________
7. In what year was the Twenty-Seventh Amendment ratified? ____________________
8. If Congress makes a law that affects a congressperson's pay, when does that law take effect? ____________________
9. According to the Fourteenth Amendment, how old did a person have to be in order to vote? ____________________

ANSWERS

1. poll tax
2. money that must be paid in order to vote
3. vice president
4. 18
5. written letters
6. 21
7. 1992
8. beginning of the next term
9. 21

LESSON 23

pending and unratified amendments

I confess that there are several parts of this Constitution which I do not at present approve, but I am not sure I shall never approve them. For having lived long, I have experienced many instances of being obliged by better information, or fuller consideration, to change opinions even on important subjects, which I once thought right, but found to be otherwise.

—Benjamin Franklin

This lesson explores some amendments that have been proposed over the years, but were never ratified. You will learn which ones are still outstanding and which ones have expired, as well as why these particular amendments never made it into the Constitution.

ARTICLE 5 OF the original text of the Constitution, written by the Founding Fathers, explains that in order for an amendment to be added to the Constitution, three-fourths of the states must agree. Since there are now 50 states, when an amendment is proposed, 38 of the 50 must agree for it to get ratified. Sometimes this doesn't happen. Some of the following proposed amendments do not currently have the required 38 states on board, but since they don't have expiration dates, they are still technically pending and could possibly become amendments in the future. Other proposed amendments never got ratified because they came with an expiration date that has since expired.

Either way, each of the following proposed amendments has not made it into the Constitution.

NUMBER OF REPRESENTATIVES AMENDMENT

When the Bill of Rights was proposed in 1789, it consisted of 12 amendments, not 10. As you know, 10 of the proposed 12 became the Bill of Rights and one of the ones originally not included was ratified in 1992 as the Twenty-seventh Amendment. So what happened to that last proposed amendment? It is still pending, since it has no expiration date, but it has yet to become a part of the Constitution.

The reason this amendment has yet to be ratified is, in part, because it is no longer relevant today. The proposed amendment declared that once the number of members of the House of Representatives reached 100, then it should not fall below 100. Once the number reached 200 members, it should not fall below 200. Today, the House of Representatives has more than 400 members, so adding an amendment stating that the number of members cannot go below 200 is essentially *moot*.

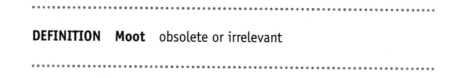

DEFINITION **Moot** obsolete or irrelevant

ANTI-TITLE AMENDMENT

This amendment was proposed in 1810 and, since it, too, has no expiration date, technically it is still awaiting ratification and could someday still be added to the Constitution, although this is very unlikely. *Anti-Title* refers to the title given to someone of nobility (like a king, a queen, or a duke). The proposed amendment takes away the citizenship of anyone who accepts a title of nobility from a foreign government or accepts a gift from a foreign government without the consent of Congress.

SLAVERY AMENDMENT

Proposed at the beginning of the Civil War in 1861, this amendment was a product of its time in history. Slavery would not be found unconstitutional until the ratification of the Thirteenth Amendment in 1865, and in 1861 there were still many people who wanted to hold onto their slaves. To satisfy those people and to prevent the Civil War, Thomas Corwin, a representative from Ohio, proposed the following amendment—which, like the previous two, is still outstanding:

> No amendment shall be made to the Constitution which will authorize or give to Congress the power to abolish or interfere, within any State, with the domestic institutions thereof, including that of persons held to labor or service by the laws of said State.

You can see that the amendment would prohibit Congress from making any laws that interfered with the domestic institutions of any state, meaning that Congress would not be able to abolish slavery. Four years after this amendment was proposed, the Thirteenth Amendment was ratified, abolishing slavery in the United States and its territories, so Corwin's proposal became moot.

CHILD LABOR AMENDMENT

In 1926 an amendment was proposed that would grant Congress the power to regulate the labor of children under the age of 18. It has no expiration date and is still outstanding.

There are two problems with this amendment that prevented it from being ratified. One is the age. Many people felt that 17 and 18 year olds were old enough to work and that the age in the amendment should be 16. The second problem is the word *labor*. Notice that "labor" is used instead of "employment." Some complained about this, asking how a person defined *labor*. Is a child doing the dishes open to regulation by Congress? What about a boy helping his father on their farm? *Employment* would have implied that the child was being paid for his or her services, but *labor* is much trickier to define. This confusion and debate helped prevent the ratification of this amendment.

EQUAL RIGHTS AMENDMENT

Section 1 of the proposed Equal Rights Amendment (the ERA) says that

> Equality of rights under the law shall not be denied or abridged by the United States or by any State on account of sex.

Sounds pretty good, right? Well, the amendment was proposed in 1972, had an expiration date of seven years that was extended to 10 years, and then expired in 1982. But why wasn't it added to the Constitution?

On first thought, the Equal Rights Amendment seems like a good idea, but there were reasons why it never gained enough support to be ratified. Some argued that the amendment seemed silly, because, since securing the right to vote in 1920, women were already entitled to all the same rights as men were under the Constitution. Others (mainly women) argued that perhaps equality under the law wasn't what they wanted. Equality under the law would mean that women, along with men, would be eligible for a draft and made to fight in the military. Equality under the law also meant that in cases involving child custody, men would be thought of as equal to women, and this might not be advantageous to women fighting for the right to raise their children. The debate dragged on for 10 years and supporters never obtained the agreement of enough states to ratify the amendment.

WASHINGTON, DC VOTING RIGHTS AMENDMENT

Remember how the Twenty-Third Amendment granted citizens of Washington, DC the right to vote for president? This amendment, proposed in 1978, would have granted citizens of Washington, DC full representation in Congress. It did not gain enough support in the seven-year period allotted for its ratification, and it expired in 1985.

Of the amendments that are still pending ratification, which do you think should be ratified? Why? Explain to a family member your argument in support of the amendment.

PRACTICE 1

Decide whether each of the following statements is *true* or *false*.

1. Twenty-eight states are needed to ratify an amendment.

2. Some proposed amendments have expired, while others are still pending ratification.

3. The Number of Representatives Amendment was originally proposed as part of the Bill of Rights.

4. There are more than 400 members of the House of Representatives.

5. The Anti-Title Amendment would fine people for accepting a title of nobility from a foreign government.

6. Thomas Corwin was an abolitionist.

7. In the wording of the proposed Child Labor Amendment, some thought that the term *labor* was too general.

8. In some ways, women did not want to be treated equally under the law.

9. Citizens of Washington, DC are not allowed to vote for president.

10. Amendments that are still pending could possibly become part of the Constitution in the future.

ANSWERS

1. **false.** Thirty-eight states, or three-fourths of the states, have to agree in order for an amendment to be ratified.
2. **true.**
3. **true.**
4. **true.**
5. **false.** The Anti-Title Amendment would take away the citizenship of anyone who accepts a title of nobility from a foreign government.
6. **false.** Thomas Corwin proposed the unratified Slavery Amendment, which would have prohibited Congress from making slavery illegal, to prevent the Civil War.
7. **true.**
8. **true.**
9. **false.** Citizens of Washington, DC are allowed to vote for president, but they are not represented in Congress.
10. **true.**

POSTTEST

CONGRATULATIONS ON MAKING it through all the lessons in this book! The following test is designed to reveal how much you've learned along the way. Like the Pretest, it consists of 30 questions, some multiple choice, some matching, some fill-in-the-blank, and some True or False. It should take you about 30 minutes to complete. You'll find all the answers at the end, along with the lesson number where each answer can be found. Good luck!

Choose the best answer to the following questions.

1. What happened at the Constitutional Convention?
   a. The Revolutionary War began.
   b. The Declaration of Independence was written.
   c. The Constitution was scrapped.
   d. The Constitution was written.

2. Which Founder was an Anti-Federalist?
  a. James Madison
  b. Alexander Hamilton
  c. both of the above
  d. neither of the above

3. Why was the Constitution written?
  a. to create a government
  b. to declare colonists' resentment toward Britain
  c. to declare independence from Britain
  d. to declare war on Britain

4. Which Founder did not attend the Constitutional Convention?
  a. George Washington
  b. Thomas Jefferson
  c. Benjamin Franklin
  d. none of the above

5. Why did the Founders think it was important to have a separation of powers in the government?
  a. so that they would win the Revolutionary War
  b. so that George Washington would be the first president
  c. so no single branch of government becomes too powerful
  d. so they could punish the British

Match each term with its definition.

6. Women's Movement	**a.** lawmaking body of the federal government
7. Senator	**b.** when a government official is elected by the citizens, not members of the government
8. emancipation	**c.** to make alcohol illegally
9. bootleg	**d.** the counting of something
10. direct election	**e.** having to do with the government of the United States
11. federal	**f.** person either born in the United States or naturalized

12. citizen
13. Congress
14. repeal
15. enumeration

g. to take back
h. the freeing of slaves
i. member of the Senate
j. movement for women's suffrage

Fill in the blank with the appropriate number.

16. The _____ Amendment bans alcohol.

17. The _____ Amendment secures freedom of the press.

18. The _____ Amendment calls for the direct election of Senators.

19. The _____ Amendment secures the right to trial by jury in civil cases.

20. The _____ Amendment protects against unreasonable searches and seizures.

21. The _____ Amendment states that the power of the federal government is limited to what is spelled out in the Constitution.

22. The _____ Amendment abolishes slavery.

23. The _____ Amendment secures due process of law against the federal government.

24. The _____ Amendment secures the right for women to vote.

25. The _____ Amendment limits the president to two terms in office.

Decide whether each of the following statements is *true* or *false*.

26. Thirty of the 50 states need to agree in order for an amendment to be ratified.

27. The federal government consists of three branches.

28. The Preamble is at the end of the Constitution.

29. Members of the House of Representatives must be at least thirty years old.

30. The President is commander in chief of the armed forces.

ANSWERS

1. **d** (Lesson 1)
2. **d** (Lesson 4)
3. **a** (Lesson 1)
4. **b** (Lesson 2)
5. **c** (Lesson 3)
6. **j** (Lesson 20)
7. **i** (Lesson 3)
8. **h** (Lesson 15)
9. **c** (Lesson 19)
10. **b** (Lesson 18)
11. **e** (Lesson 3)
12. **f** (Lesson 16)
13. **a** (Lesson 6)
14. **g** (Lesson 19)
15. **d** (Lesson 16)
16. **18** (Lesson 19)
17. **1** (Lesson 8)
18. **17** (Lesson 18)
19. **7** (Lesson 12)
20. **4** (Lesson 10)
21. **10** (Lesson 13)
22. **13** (Lesson 15)
23. **5** (Lesson 11)
24. **19** (Lesson 20)
25. **22** (Lesson 21)
26. **false.** Thirty-eight of 50 states have to agree in order for an amendment to become part of the Constitution. (Lesson 7)
27. **true** (Lesson 3)
28. **false.** The Preamble is the introduction to the Constitution and is at the beginning. (Lesson 5)
29. **false.** In order to be a member of the House of Representatives, a person must be at least twenty-five years old. (Lesson 6)
30. **true** (Lesson 7)

APPENDICES

APPENDIX A

glossary

abolitionist someone who supported the elimination of slavery in the United States

ambassador someone who officially represents their country while living in that country

amendment part of the Constitution that was added onto the original text

Anti-Federalist a person who, during the debate about the Constitution, believed that the federal government was given too much power and infringed upon the rights of the citizens

articles parts of the original text of the Constitution

Articles of Confederation document created by the First Continental Congress that was designed to set up a basic structure of governing for the newly independent states

Bill of Rights the first 10 Amendments to the Constitution

bootleg to make and sell alcohol illegally during Prohibition

cabinet the president's advisory body

candidate a person who is running for election to a position in the government

checks and balances system by which each branch of the federal government has limited powers in order for no one branch to overtake the others

citizen a person who is either born in the United States or legally becomes entitled to all the privileges and rights given by the Constitution of the United States

Civil War a war that took place between 1861 and 1865 in the United States between the Southern states that had left the Union and the Northern states that had remained

Confederate a person who supported the Southern states that had left the Union before the Civil War

Congress the lawmaking body of the federal government, consisting of the Senate and the House of Representatives

Constitution the document, written by the Founders and added to over the years, which declares the rights of U.S. citizens, explains how the federal government of the country will operate and on which the United States was founded

Constitutional Convention meeting in Philadelphia in 1787 at which the Founders created and approved the country's Constitution

direct election when a government official is elected by the citizens of the state or country

double jeopardy to be put on trial twice for the same crime

elector a person who votes for a government official, acting as a representative for citizens

Electoral College the system by which the president is elected

elitism thinking of oneself as being better in some way than other people

emancipation the freeing of slaves from bondage

eminent domain the right of the federal government to seize private property for public use, if proper compensation is offered

enumeration the counting of something, usually in the case of the population of a state or country

federal having to do with the central government of the United States

federalism the belief that a strong, powerful federal government is most effective

federalist a person who, during the debate about the Constitution, believed that a strong, powerful central government was best

Federalist Papers a collection of essays secretly written by James Madison, Alexander Hamilton, and John Jay that were distributed around the country in 1788 in order to persuade the public to ratify the Constitution

Founders the men who are credited with creating the original text of the Constitution

grand jury a jury that decides whether there is enough evidence for a case to go to trial

House of Representatives part of Congress that consists of state representatives; the number is elected based on the population of the state

involuntary servitude forced labor

judicial having to do with the justice system of the United States

lame duck a president who is still in office, but who is not serving another term

legislature the lawmaking branch of the United States government

militia a group of citizens acting in a military capacity

naturalized citizen a person who was not born in the United States, but who becomes a citizen through a legal process

New Jersey Plan during the Constitutional debate, a plan proposed by the delegates from New Jersey in which there would be a single house of Congress, with each state getting one vote

Noble Experiment another name for the period in United States history during which the manufacture, sale, and transport of alcohol was banned (also known as **Prohibition**)

Plead the Fifth to use the right that is given to you by the Fifth Amendment, to not incriminate yourself in court

poll tax a fee that is required in order to vote

Preamble introduction to the Constitution

Prohibition name for the period in United States history during which the manufacture, sale, and transport of alcohol was banned (also known as **The Noble Experiment**)

ratification when an amendment is officially added to the Constitution

repeal to take back or undo, as in the case of the Eighteenth Amendment and the Twenty-First Amendment

salutary neglect policy under which the British government left the colonies alone, as long as everything was going well

Senate part of Congress that consists of two representatives from each state, regardless of the population of that state

separation of powers the idea that no one branch of government will have supreme power over another

sovereignty having supreme power

speakeasy a secret establishment that served alcohol illegally during Prohibition

suffrage the right to vote

Supreme Court highest court in the federal judicial system

The Union the term used to refer to the United States, especially to the northern states during the Civil War

three-fifths clause the part of the Constitution that states that for the purposes of representation in the federal government, slaves would count as three-fifths of a person

treason when a government official knowingly undermines the government of the United States

Virginia plan during the Constitutional debate, a plan proposed by the delegates from Virginia in which there would be two houses of government, each consisting of representatives from each state based on the population of that state

warrant document needed in order for law enforcement officers to administer a search or seizure

Women's Movement a movement whose supporters believed that women should have equal rights to men, especially the right to vote

APPENDIX **B**

the full text of the constitution, bill of rights, and the amendments

PREAMBLE

WE THE PEOPLE of the United States, in order to form a more perfect union, establish Justice, insure domestic tranquility, provide for the common defence, promote the general Welfare, and secure the Blessings of Liberty to ourselves and our Posterity, do ordain and establish this Constitution for the United States of America.

Article I

Section 1

All legislative Powers herein granted shall be vested in a Congress of the United States, which shall consist of a Senate and a House of Representatives.

Section 2

The House of Representatives shall be composed of Members chosen every second Year by the People of the several States, and the Electors in each State shall have the Qualifications requisite for Electors of the most numerous Branch of the State Legislature.

No Person shall be a Representative who shall not have attained to the Age of twenty five Years, and been seven Years a Citizen of the United States, and who shall not, when elected, be an Inhabitant of that State in which he shall be chosen.

Representatives and direct Taxes shall be apportioned among the several States which may be included within this Union, according to their respective Numbers, which shall be determined by adding to the whole Number of free Persons, including those bound to Service for a Term of Years, and excluding Indians not taxed, three fifths of all other Persons. The actual Enumeration shall be made within three Years after the first Meeting of the Congress of the United States, and within every subsequent Term of ten Years, in such Manner as they shall by Law direct. The Number of Representatives shall not exceed one for every thirty Thousand, but each State shall have at Least one Representative; and until such enumeration shall be made, the State of New Hampshire shall be entitled to chuse three, Massachusetts eight, Rhode-Island and Providence Plantations one, Connecticut five, New-York six, New Jersey four, Pennsylvania eight, Delaware one, Maryland six, Virginia ten, North Carolina five, South Carolina five, and Georgia three.

When vacancies happen in the Representation from any State, the Executive Authority thereof shall issue Writs of Election to fill such Vacancies.

The House of Representatives shall chuse their Speaker and other Officers; and shall have the sole Power of Impeachment.

Section 3

The Senate of the United States shall be composed of two Senators from each State, chosen by the Legislature thereof, for six Years; and each Senator shall have one Vote.

Immediately after they shall be assembled in Consequence of the first Election, they shall be divided as equally as may be into three Classes. The Seats of the Senators of the first Class shall be vacated at the Expiration of the second Year, of the second Class at the Expiration of the fourth Year, and of the third Class at the Expiration of the sixth Year, so that one third may be chosen every second Year; and if Vacancies happen by Resignation, or otherwise, during the Recess of the Legislature of any State, the Executive thereof may make temporary Appointments until the next Meeting of the Legislature, which shall then fill such Vacancies.

No Person shall be a Senator who shall not have attained to the Age of thirty Years, and been nine Years a Citizen of the United States, and who shall not, when elected, be an Inhabitant of that State for which he shall be chosen.

The Vice President of the United States shall be President of the Senate, but shall have no Vote, unless they be equally divided.

The Senate shall chuse their other Officers, and also a President pro tempore, in the Absence of the Vice President, or when he shall exercise the Office of President of the United States.

The Senate shall have the sole Power to try all Impeachments. When sitting for that Purpose, they shall be on Oath or Affirmation. When the President of the United States is tried, the Chief Justice shall preside: And no Person shall be convicted without the Concurrence of two thirds of the Members present.

Judgment in Cases of Impeachment shall not extend further than to removal from Office, and disqualification to hold and enjoy any Office of honor, Trust or Profit under the United States: but the Party convicted shall nevertheless be liable and subject to Indictment, Trial, Judgment and Punishment, according to Law.

Section 4

The Times, Places and Manner of holding Elections for Senators and Representatives, shall be prescribed in each State by the Legislature thereof; but the Congress may at any time by Law make or alter such Regulations, except as to the Places of chusing Senators.

The Congress shall assemble at least once in every Year, and such Meeting shall be on the first Monday in December, unless they shall by Law appoint a different Day.

Section 5

Each House shall be the Judge of the Elections, Returns and Qualifications of its own Members, and a Majority of each shall constitute a Quorum to do Business; but a smaller Number may adjourn from day to day, and may be authorized to compel the Attendance of absent Members, in such Manner, and under such Penalties as each House may provide.

Each House may determine the Rules of its Proceedings, punish its Members for disorderly Behaviour, and, with the Concurrence of two thirds, expel a Member.

Each House shall keep a Journal of its Proceedings, and from time to time publish the same, excepting such Parts as may in their Judgment require Secrecy; and the Yeas and Nays of the Members of either House on any question shall, at the Desire of one fifth of those Present, be entered on the Journal.

Neither House, during the Session of Congress, shall, without the Consent of the other, adjourn for more than three days, nor to any other Place than that in which the two Houses shall be sitting.

Section 6

The Senators and Representatives shall receive a Compensation for their Services, to be ascertained by Law, and paid out of the Treasury of the United States. They shall in all Cases, except Treason, Felony and Breach of the Peace, be privileged from Arrest during their Attendance at the Session of their respective Houses, and in going to and returning from the same; and for any Speech or Debate in either House, they shall not be questioned in any other Place.

No Senator or Representative shall, during the Time for which he was elected, be appointed to any civil Office under the Authority of the United States, which shall have been created, or the Emoluments whereof shall have been encreased during such time; and no Person holding any Office under the United States, shall be a Member of either House during his Continuance in Office.

Section 7

All Bills for raising Revenue shall originate in the House of Representatives; but the Senate may propose or concur with Amendments as on other Bills.

Every Bill which shall have passed the House of Representatives and the Senate, shall, before it become a Law, be presented to the President of the United States; If he approves he shall sign it, but if not he shall return it, with his Objections to that House in which it shall have originated, who shall enter the Objections at large on their Journal, and proceed to reconsider it. If after such Reconsideration two thirds of that House shall agree to pass the Bill, it shall be sent, together with the Objections, to the other House, by which it shall likewise be reconsidered, and if approved by two thirds of that House, it shall become a Law. But in all such Cases the Votes of both Houses shall be determined by Yeas and Nays, and the Names of the Persons voting for and against the Bill shall be entered on the Journal of each House respectively. If any Bill shall not be returned by the President within ten Days (Sundays excepted) after it shall have been presented to him, the Same shall be a Law, in like Manner as if he had signed it, unless the Congress by their Adjournment prevent its Return, in which Case it shall not be a Law.

Every Order, Resolution, or Vote to which the Concurrence of the Senate and House of Representatives may be necessary (except on a question of Adjournment) shall be presented to the President of the United States; and before the Same shall take Effect, shall be approved by him, or being disapproved by him, shall be repassed by two thirds of the Senate and House of Representatives, according to the Rules and Limitations prescribed in the Case of a Bill.

Section 8

The Congress shall have Power To lay and collect Taxes, Duties, Imposts and Excises, to pay the Debts and provide for the common Defence and general Welfare of the United States; but all Duties, Imposts and Excises shall be uniform throughout the United States;

To borrow Money on the credit of the United States;

To regulate Commerce with foreign Nations, and among the several States, and with the Indian Tribes;

To establish an uniform Rule of Naturalization, and uniform Laws on the subject of Bankruptcies throughout the United States;

To coin Money, regulate the Value thereof, and of foreign Coin, and fix the Standard of Weights and Measures;

To provide for the Punishment of counterfeiting the Securities and current Coin of the United States;

To establish Post Offices and post Roads;

To promote the Progress of Science and useful Arts, by securing for limited Times to Authors and Inventors the exclusive Right to their respective Writings and Discoveries;

To constitute Tribunals inferior to the supreme Court;

To define and punish Piracies and Felonies committed on the high Seas, and Offences against the Law of Nations;

To declare War, grant Letters of Marque and Reprisal, and make Rules concerning Captures on Land and Water;

To raise and support Armies, but no Appropriation of Money to that Use shall be for a longer Term than two Years;

To provide and maintain a Navy;

To make Rules for the Government and Regulation of the land and naval Forces;

To provide for calling forth the Militia to execute the Laws of the Union, suppress Insurrections and repel Invasions;

To provide for organizing, arming, and disciplining the Militia, and for governing such Part of them as may be employed in the Service of the United

States, reserving to the States respectively, the Appointment of the Officers, and the Authority of training the Militia according to the discipline prescribed by Congress;

To exercise exclusive Legislation in all Cases whatsoever, over such District (not exceeding ten Miles square) as may, by Cession of particular States, and the Acceptance of Congress, become the Seat of the Government of the United States, and to exercise like Authority over all Places purchased by the Consent of the Legislature of the State in which the Same shall be, for the Erection of Forts, Magazines, Arsenals, dock-Yards, and other needful Buildings;—And

To make all Laws which shall be necessary and proper for carrying into Execution the foregoing Powers, and all other Powers vested by this Constitution in the Government of the United States, or in any Department or Officer thereof.

Section 9

The Migration or Importation of such Persons as any of the States now existing shall think proper to admit, shall not be prohibited by the Congress prior to the Year one thousand eight hundred and eight, but a Tax or duty may be imposed on such Importation, not exceeding ten dollars for each Person.

The Privilege of the Writ of Habeas Corpus shall not be suspended, unless when in Cases of Rebellion or Invasion the public Safety may require it.

No Bill of Attainder or ex post facto Law shall be passed.

No Capitation, or other direct, Tax shall be laid, unless in Proportion to the Census or enumeration herein before directed to be taken.

No Tax or Duty shall be laid on Articles exported from any State.

No Preference shall be given by any Regulation of Commerce or Revenue to the Ports of one State over those of another; nor shall Vessels bound to, or from, one State, be obliged to enter, clear, or pay Duties in another.

No Money shall be drawn from the Treasury, but in Consequence of Appropriations made by Law; and a regular Statement and Account of the Receipts and Expenditures of all public Money shall be published from time to time.

No Title of Nobility shall be granted by the United States: And no Person holding any Office of Profit or Trust under them, shall, without the Consent of the Congress, accept of any present, Emolument, Office, or Title, of any kind whatever, from any King, Prince, or foreign State.

Section 10

No State shall enter into any Treaty, Alliance, or Confederation; grant Letters of Marque and Reprisal; coin Money; emit Bills of Credit; make any Thing but gold and silver Coin a Tender in Payment of Debts; pass any Bill of Attainder, ex post facto Law, or Law impairing the Obligation of Contracts, or grant any Title of Nobility.

No State shall, without the Consent of the Congress, lay any Imposts or Duties on Imports or Exports, except what may be absolutely necessary for executing its inspection Laws: and the net Produce of all Duties and Imposts, laid by any State on Imports or Exports, shall be for the Use of the Treasury of the United States; and all such Laws shall be subject to the Revision and Controul of the Congress.

No State shall, without the Consent of Congress, lay any Duty of Tonnage, keep Troops, or Ships of War in time of Peace, enter into any Agreement or Compact with another State, or with a foreign Power, or engage in War, unless actually invaded, or in such imminent Danger as will not admit of delay.

Article II

Section 1

The Executive Power shall be vested in a President of the United States of America. He shall hold his Office during the Term of four Years, and, together with the Vice President, chosen for the same Term, be elected, as follows:

Each State shall appoint, in such Manner as the Legislature thereof may direct, a Number of Electors, equal to the whole Number of Senators and Representatives to which the State may be entitled in the Congress: but no Senator or Representative, or Person holding an Office of Trust or Profit under the United States, shall be appointed an Elector.

The Electors shall meet in their respective States, and vote by Ballot for two Persons, of whom one at least shall not be an Inhabitant of the same State with themselves. And they shall make a List of all the Persons voted for, and of the Number of Votes for each; which List they shall sign and certify, and transmit sealed to the Seat of the Government of the United States, directed to the President of the Senate. The President of the Senate shall, in the Presence of the Senate and House of Representatives, open all the Certificates, and the

Votes shall then be counted. The Person having the greatest Number of Votes shall be the President, if such Number be a Majority of the whole Number of Electors appointed; and if there be more than one who have such Majority, and have an equal Number of Votes, then the House of Representatives shall immediately chuse by Ballot one of them for President; and if no Person have a Majority, then from the five highest on the List the said House shall in like Manner chuse the President. But in chusing the President, the Votes shall be taken by States, the Representation from each State having one Vote; A quorum for this purpose shall consist of a Member or Members from two thirds of the States, and a Majority of all the States shall be necessary to a Choice. In every Case, after the Choice of the President, the Person having the greatest Number of Votes of the Electors shall be the Vice President. But if there should remain two or more who have equal Votes, the Senate shall chuse from them by Ballot the Vice President.

The Congress may determine the Time of chusing the Electors, and the Day on which they shall give their Votes; which Day shall be the same throughout the United States.

No Person except a natural born Citizen, or a Citizen of the United States, at the time of the Adoption of this Constitution, shall be eligible to the Office of President; neither shall any Person be eligible to that Office who shall not have attained to the Age of thirty five Years, and been fourteen Years a Resident within the United States.

In Case of the Removal of the President from Office, or of his Death, Resignation, or Inability to discharge the Powers and Duties of the said Office, the same shall devolve on the Vice President, and the Congress may by Law provide for the Case of Removal, Death, Resignation or Inability, both of the President and Vice President, declaring what Officer shall then act as President, and such Officer shall act accordingly, until the Disability be removed, or a President shall be elected.

The President shall, at stated Times, receive for his Services, a Compensation, which shall neither be encreased nor diminished during the Period for which he shall have been elected, and he shall not receive within that Period any other Emolument from the United States, or any of them.

Before he enter on the Execution of his Office, he shall take the following Oath or Affirmation:—"I do solemnly swear (or affirm) that I will faithfully execute the Office of President of the United States, and will to the best of my Ability, preserve, protect and defend the Constitution of the United States."

Section 2

The President shall be Commander in Chief of the Army and Navy of the United States, and of the Militia of the several States, when called into the actual Service of the United States; he may require the Opinion, in writing, of the principal Officer in each of the executive Departments, upon any Subject relating to the Duties of their respective Offices, and he shall have Power to grant Reprieves and Pardons for Offences against the United States, except in Cases of Impeachment.

He shall have Power, by and with the Advice and Consent of the Senate, to make Treaties, provided two thirds of the Senators present concur and he shall nominate, and by and with the Advice and Consent of the Senate, shall appoint Ambassadors, other public Ministers and Consuls, Judges of the supreme Court, and all other Officers of the United States, whose Appointments are not herein otherwise provided for, and which shall be established by Law: but the Congress may by Law vest the Appointment of such inferior Officers, as they think proper, in the President alone, in the Courts of Law, or in the Heads of Departments.

The President shall have Power to fill up all Vacancies that may happen during the Recess of the Senate, by granting Commissions which shall expire at the End of their next Session.

Section 3

He shall from time to time give to the Congress Information of the State of the Union, and recommend to their Consideration such Measures as he shall judge necessary and expedient; he may, on extraordinary Occasions, convene both Houses, or either of them, and, in Case of Disagreement between them, with Respect to the Time of Adjournment, he may adjourn them to such Time as he shall think proper; he shall receive Ambassadors and other public Ministers; he shall take Care that the Laws be faithfully executed, and shall Commission all the Officers of the United States.

Section 4

The President, Vice President and all civil Officers of the United States, shall be removed from Office on Impeachment for, and Conviction of, Treason, Bribery, or other high Crimes and Misdemeanors.

Article III

Section 1

The judicial Power of the United States, shall be vested in one supreme Court, and in such inferior Courts as the Congress may from time to time ordain and establish. The Judges, both of the supreme and inferior Courts, shall hold their Offices during good Behaviour, and shall, at stated Times, receive for their Services, a Compensation, which shall not be diminished during their Continuance in Office.

Section 2

The judicial Power shall extend to all Cases, in Law and Equity, arising under this Constitution, the Laws of the United States, and Treaties made, or which shall be made, under their Authority;—to all Cases affecting Ambassadors, other public Ministers and Consuls;—to all Cases of admiralty and maritime Jurisdiction;—to Controversies to which the United States shall be a Party;—to Controversies between two or more States;— between a State and Citizens of another State,—between Citizens of different States;—between Citizens of the same State claiming Lands under Grants of different States, and between a State, or the Citizens thereof, and foreign States, Citizens or Subjects.

In all Cases affecting Ambassadors, other public Ministers and Consuls, and those in which a State shall be Party, the supreme Court shall have original Jurisdiction. In all the other Cases before mentioned, the supreme Court shall have appellate Jurisdiction, both as to Law and Fact, with such Exceptions, and under such Regulations as the Congress shall make.

The Trial of all Crimes, except in Cases of Impeachment, shall be by Jury; and such Trial shall be held in the State where the said Crimes shall have been committed; but when not committed within any State, the Trial shall be at such Place or Places as the Congress may by Law have directed.

Section 3

Treason against the United States, shall consist only in levying War against them, or in adhering to their Enemies, giving them Aid and Comfort. No Person shall be convicted of Treason unless on the Testimony of two Witnesses to the same overt Act, or on Confession in open Court.

The Congress shall have Power to declare the Punishment of Treason, but no Attainder of Treason shall work Corruption of Blood, or Forfeiture except during the Life of the Person attainted.

Article IV

Section 1

Full Faith and Credit shall be given in each State to the public Acts, Records, and judicial Proceedings of every other State. And the Congress may by general Laws prescribe the Manner in which such Acts, Records and Proceedings shall be proved, and the Effect thereof.

Section 2

The Citizens of each State shall be entitled to all Privileges and Immunities of Citizens in the several States.

A Person charged in any State with Treason, Felony, or other Crime, who shall flee from Justice, and be found in another State, shall on Demand of the executive Authority of the State from which he fled, be delivered up, to be removed to the State having Jurisdiction of the Crime.

No Person held to Service or Labour in one State, under the Laws thereof, escaping into another, shall, in Consequence of any Law or Regulation therein, be discharged from such Service or Labour, but shall be delivered up on Claim of the Party to whom such Service or Labour may be due.

Section 3

New States may be admitted by the Congress into this Union; but no new State shall be formed or erected within the Jurisdiction of any other State; nor any State be formed by the Junction of two or more States, or Parts of States, without the Consent of the Legislatures of the States concerned as well as of the Congress.

The Congress shall have Power to dispose of and make all needful Rules and Regulations respecting the Territory or other Property belonging to the United States; and nothing in this Constitution shall be so construed as to Prejudice any Claims of the United States, or of any particular State.

Section 4

The United States shall guarantee to every State in this Union a Republican Form of Government, and shall protect each of them against Invasion; and on Application of the Legislature, or of the Executive (when the Legislature cannot be convened) against domestic Violence.

Article V

The Congress, whenever two thirds of both Houses shall deem it necessary, shall propose Amendments to this Constitution, or, on the Application of the Legislatures of two thirds of the several States, shall call a Convention for proposing Amendments, which, in either Case, shall be valid to all Intents and Purposes, as Part of this Constitution, when ratified by the Legislatures of three fourths of the several States, or by Conventions in three fourths thereof, as the one or the other Mode of Ratification may be proposed by the Congress; Provided that no Amendment which may be made prior to the Year One thousand eight hundred and eight shall in any Manner affect the first and fourth Clauses in the Ninth Section of the first Article; and that no State, without its Consent, shall be deprived of its equal Suffrage in the Senate.

Article VI

All Debts contracted and Engagements entered into, before the Adoption of this Constitution, shall be as valid against the United States under this Constitution, as under the Confederation.

This Constitution, and the Laws of the United States which shall be made in Pursuance thereof; and all Treaties made, or which shall be made, under the Authority of the United States, shall be the supreme Law of the Land; and the Judges in every State shall be bound thereby, any Thing in the Constitution or Laws of any State to the Contrary notwithstanding.

The Senators and Representatives before mentioned, and the Members of the several State Legislatures, and all executive and judicial Officers, both of the United States and of the several States, shall be bound by Oath or Affirmation, to support this Constitution; but no religious Test shall ever be required as a Qualification to any Office or public Trust under the United States.

Article VII

The Ratification of the Conventions of nine States, shall be sufficient for the Establishment of this Constitution between the States so ratifying the Same.
DONE in Convention by the Unanimous Consent of the States present the Seventeenth Day of September in the Year of our Lord one thousand seven hun-

dred and Eighty seven and of the Independence of the United States of America the Twelfth. IN WITNESS whereof We have hereunto subscribed our Names.

George Washington—President and deputy from **Virginia**

New Hampshire: John Langdon, Nicholas Gilman
Massachusetts: Nathaniel Gorham, Rufus King
Connecticut: William Samuel Johnson, Roger Sherman
New York: Alexander Hamilton
New Jersey: William Livingston, David Brearly, William Paterson, Jonathan Dayton
Pennsylvania: Benjamin Franklin, Thomas Mifflin, Robert Morris, George Clymer, Thomas FitzSimons, Jared Ingersoll, James Wilson, Gouverneur Morris
Delaware: George Read, Gunning Bedford, Jr., John Dickinson, Richard Bassett, Jacob Broom
Maryland: James McHenry, Daniel of Saint Thomas Jenifer, Daniel Carroll
Virginia: John Blair, James Madison, Jr.
North Carolina: William Blount, Richard Dobbs Spaight, Hugh Williamson
South Carolina: John Rutledge, Charles Cotesworth Pinckney, Charles Pinckney, Pierce Butler
Georgia: William Few, Abraham Baldwin

THE BILL OF RIGHTS

The Preamble to The Bill of Rights

Congress of the United States begun and held at the City of New-York, on Wednesday the fourth of March, one thousand seven hundred and eighty nine.

THE Conventions of a number of the States, having at the time of their adopting the Constitution, expressed a desire, in order to prevent misconstruction or abuse of its powers, that further declaratory and restrictive clauses should be added: And as extending the ground of public confidence in the Government, will best ensure the beneficent ends of its institution.

RESOLVED by the Senate and House of Representatives of the United States of America, in Congress assembled, two thirds of both Houses concurring, that the following Articles be proposed to the Legislatures of the several States, as amendments to the Constitution of the United States, all, or any of which Articles, when ratified by three fourths of the said Legislatures, to be valid to all intents and purposes, as part of the said Constitution; viz.

ARTICLES in addition to, and Amendment of the Constitution of the United States of America, proposed by Congress, and ratified by the Legislatures of the several States, pursuant to the fifth Article of the original Constitution.

Amendment I

Congress shall make no law respecting an establishment of religion, or prohibiting the free exercise thereof; or abridging the freedom of speech, or of the press; or the right of the people peaceably to assemble, and to petition the Government for a redress of grievances.

Amendment II

A well regulated Militia, being necessary to the security of a free State, the right of the people to keep and bear Arms, shall not be infringed.

Amendment III

No Soldier shall, in time of peace be quartered in any house, without the consent of the Owner, nor in time of war, but in a manner to be prescribed by law.

Amendment IV

The right of the people to be secure in their persons, houses, papers, and effects, against unreasonable searches and seizures, shall not be violated, and no Warrants shall issue, but upon probable cause, supported by Oath or affirmation, and particularly describing the place to be searched, and the persons or things to be seized.

Amendment V

No person shall be held to answer for a capital, or otherwise infamous crime, unless on a presentment or indictment of a Grand Jury, except in cases arising in the land or naval forces, or in the Militia, when in actual service in time of War or public danger; nor shall any person be subject for the same offence to be twice put in jeopardy of life or limb; nor shall be compelled in any criminal case to be a witness against himself, nor be deprived of life, liberty, or property, without due process of law; nor shall private property be taken for public use, without just compensation.

Amendment VI

In all criminal prosecutions, the accused shall enjoy the right to a speedy and public trial, by an impartial jury of the State and district wherein the crime shall have been committed, which district shall have been previously ascertained by law, and to be informed of the nature and cause of the accusation; to be confronted with the witnesses against him; to have compulsory process for obtaining witnesses in his favor, and to have the Assistance of Counsel for his defence.

Amendment VII

In Suits at common law, where the value in controversy shall exceed twenty dollars, the right of trial by jury shall be preserved, and no fact tried by a jury, shall be otherwise re-examined in any Court of the United States, than according to the rules of the common law.

Amendment VIII

Excessive bail shall not be required, nor excessive fines imposed, nor cruel and unusual punishments inflicted.

Amendment IX

The enumeration in the Constitution, of certain rights, shall not be construed to deny or disparage others retained by the people.

Amendment X

The powers not delegated to the United States by the Constitution, nor prohibited by it to the States, are reserved to the States respectively, or to the people.

AMENDMENTS XI–XXVII

Amendment XI

The Judicial power of the United States shall not be construed to extend to any suit in law or equity, commenced or prosecuted against one of the United States by Citizens of another State, or by Citizens or Subjects of any Foreign State.

Amendment XII

The Electors shall meet in their respective states and vote by ballot for President and Vice-President, one of whom, at least, shall not be an inhabitant of the same state with themselves; they shall name in their ballots the person voted for as President, and in distinct ballots the person voted for as Vice-President, and they shall make distinct lists of all persons voted for as President, and of all persons voted for as Vice-President, and of the number of votes for each, which lists they shall sign and certify, and transmit sealed to the seat of the government of the United States, directed to the President of the Senate; — the President of the Senate shall, in the presence of the Senate and House of Representatives, open all the certificates and the votes shall then be counted; — The person having the greatest number of votes for President, shall be the President, if such number be a majority of the whole number of Electors appointed; and if no person have such majority, then from the persons having the highest numbers not exceeding three on the list of those voted for as President, the House of Representatives shall choose immediately, by ballot, the President. But in choosing the President, the votes shall be taken by states, the representation from each state having one vote; a quorum for this purpose shall consist of a member or members from two-thirds of the states, and a majority of all the states shall be necessary to a choice. And if the House of Representatives shall not choose a President whenever the right of choice shall devolve upon them, before the fourth day of March next following, then the Vice-President shall act as President, as in the case of the death or other constitutional disability of the President. The person having the greatest number of votes as Vice-President, shall be the Vice-President, if such number be a majority of the whole number of Electors appointed, and if no person have a majority, then from the two highest numbers on the list, the Senate shall choose the Vice-President; a quorum for the purpose shall consist of two-thirds of the whole number of Senators, and a majority of the whole number shall be necessary to a choice. But no person constitutionally ineligible to the office of President shall be eligible to that of Vice-President of the United States.

Amendment XIII

Section 1

Neither slavery nor involuntary servitude, except as a punishment for crime whereof the party shall have been duly convicted, shall exist within the United States, or any place subject to their jurisdiction.

Section 2

Congress shall have power to enforce this article by appropriate legislation.

Amendment XIV

Section 1

All persons born or naturalized in the United States, and subject to the jurisdiction thereof, are citizens of the United States and of the State wherein they reside. No State shall make or enforce any law which shall abridge the privileges or immunities of citizens of the United States; nor shall any State deprive any person of life, liberty, or property, without due process of law; nor deny to any person within its jurisdiction the equal protection of the laws.

Section 2

Representatives shall be apportioned among the several States according to their respective numbers, counting the whole number of persons in each State, excluding Indians not taxed. But when the right to vote at any election for the choice of electors for President and Vice-President of the United States, Representatives in Congress, the Executive and Judicial officers of a State, or the members of the Legislature thereof, is denied to any of the male inhabitants of such State, being twenty-one years of age, and citizens of the United States, or in any way abridged, except for participation in rebellion, or other crime, the basis of representation therein shall be reduced in the proportion which the number of such male citizens shall bear to the whole number of male citizens twenty-one years of age in such State.

Section 3

No person shall be a Senator or Representative in Congress, or elector of President and Vice-President, or hold any office, civil or military, under the United States, or under any State, who, having previously taken an oath, as a member of Congress, or as an officer of the United States, or as a member of any State legislature, or as an executive or judicial officer of any State, to support the Constitution of the United States, shall have engaged in insurrection or rebellion against the same, or given aid or comfort to the enemies thereof. But Congress may by a vote of two-thirds of each House, remove such disability.

Section 4

The validity of the public debt of the United States, authorized by law, including debts incurred for payment of pensions and bounties for services in suppressing insurrection or rebellion, shall not be questioned. But neither the United States nor any State shall assume or pay any debt or obligation incurred in aid of insurrection or rebellion against the United States, or any claim for the loss or emancipation of any slaves; but all such debts, obligations, and claims shall be held illegal and void.

Section 5

The Congress shall have power to enforce, by appropriate legislation, the provisions of this article.

Amendment XV

Section 1

The right of citizens of the United States to vote shall not be denied or abridged by the United States or by any State on account of race, color, or previous condition of servitude.

Section 2

The Congress shall have power to enforce this article by appropriate legislation.

Amendment XVI

The Congress shall have power to lay and collect taxes on incomes, from whatever source derived, without apportionment among the several States, and without regard to any census or enumeration.

Amendment XVII

The Senate of the United States shall be composed of two Senators from each State, elected by the people thereof, for six years; and each Senator shall have one vote. The electors in each State shall have the qualifications requisite for electors of the most numerous branch of the State legislatures.

When vacancies happen in the representation of any State in the Senate, the executive authority of such State shall issue writs of election to fill such vacancies: Provided, That the legislature of any State may empower the executive thereof to make temporary appointments until the people fill the vacancies by election as the legislature may direct.

This amendment shall not be so construed as to affect the election or term of any Senator chosen before it becomes valid as part of the Constitution.

Amendment XVIII

Section 1

After one year from the ratification of this article the manufacture, sale, or transportation of intoxicating liquors within, the importation thereof into, or the exportation thereof from the United States and all territory subject to the jurisdiction thereof for beverage purposes is hereby prohibited.

Section 2

The Congress and the several States shall have concurrent power to enforce this article by appropriate legislation.

Section 3

This article shall be inoperative unless it shall have been ratified as an amendment to the Constitution by the legislatures of the several States, as provided in the Constitution, within seven years from the date of the submission hereof to the States by the Congress.

Amendment XIX

Section 1

The right of citizens of the United States to vote shall not be denied or abridged by the United States or by any State on account of sex.

Section 2

Congress shall have power to enforce this article by appropriate legislation.

Amendment XX

Section 1

The terms of the President and the Vice President shall end at noon on the 20th day of January, and the terms of Senators and Representatives at noon on the 3rd day of January, of the years in which such terms would have ended if this article had not been ratified; and the terms of their successors shall then begin.

Section 2

The Congress shall assemble at least once in every year, and such meeting shall begin at noon on the 3rd day of January, unless they shall by law appoint a different day.

Section 3

If, at the time fixed for the beginning of the term of the President, the President elect shall have died, the Vice President elect shall become President. If a President shall not have been chosen before the time fixed for the beginning of his term, or if the President elect shall have failed to qualify, then the Vice President elect shall act as President until a President shall have qualified; and the Congress may by law provide for the case wherein neither a President elect nor a Vice President elect shall have qualified, declaring who shall then act as President, or the manner in which one who is to act shall be selected, and such person shall act accordingly until a President or Vice President shall have qualified.

Section 4

The Congress may by law provide for the case of the death of any of the persons from whom the House of Representatives may choose a President whenever the right of choice shall have devolved upon them, and for the case of the death of any of the persons from whom the Senate may choose a Vice President whenever the right of choice shall have devolved upon them.

Section 5

Sections 1 and 2 shall take effect on the 15th day of October following the ratification of this article.

Section 6

This article shall be inoperative unless it shall have been ratified as an amendment to the Constitution by the legislatures of three-fourths of the several States within seven years from the date of its submission.

Amendment XXI

Section 1

The eighteenth article of amendment to the Constitution of the United States is hereby repealed.

Section 2

The transportation or importation into any State, Territory, or possession of the United States for delivery or use therein of intoxicating liquors, in violation of the laws thereof, is hereby prohibited.

Section 3

This article shall be inoperative unless it shall have been ratified as an amendment to the Constitution by conventions in the several States, as provided in the Constitution, within seven years from the date of the submission hereof to the States by the Congress.

Amendment XXII

Section 1

No person shall be elected to the office of the President more than twice, and no person who has held the office of President, or acted as President, for more than two years of a term to which some other person was elected President shall be elected to the office of President more than once. But this article shall not apply to any person holding the office of President when this article was proposed by the Congress, and shall not prevent any person who may be holding the office of President, or acting as President, during the term within which this article becomes operative from holding the office of President or acting as President during the remainder of such term.

Section 2

This article shall be inoperative unless it shall have been ratified as an amendment to the Constitution by the legislatures of three-fourths of the several States within seven years from the date of its submission to the States by the Congress.

Amendment XXIII

Section 1

The District constituting the seat of Government of the United States shall appoint in such manner as Congress may direct:

A number of electors of President and Vice President equal to the whole number of Senators and Representatives in Congress to which the District would be entitled if it were a State, but in no event more than the least populous State; they shall be in addition to those appointed by the States, but they shall be considered, for the purposes of the election of President and Vice President, to be electors appointed by a State; and they shall meet in the District and perform such duties as provided by the twelfth article of amendment.

Section 2

The Congress shall have power to enforce this article by appropriate legislation.

Amendment XXIV

Section 1

The right of citizens of the United States to vote in any primary or other election for President or Vice President, for electors for President or Vice President, or for Senator or Representative in Congress, shall not be denied or abridged by the United States or any State by reason of failure to pay poll tax or other tax.

Section 2

The Congress shall have power to enforce this article by appropriate legislation.

Amendment XXV

Section 1

In case of the removal of the President from office or of his death or resignation, the Vice President shall become President.

Section 2

Whenever there is a vacancy in the office of the Vice President, the President shall nominate a Vice President who shall take office upon confirmation by a majority vote of both Houses of Congress.

Section 3

Whenever the President transmits to the President pro tempore of the Senate and the Speaker of the House of Representatives his written declaration that he is unable to discharge the powers and duties of his office, and until he transmits to them a written declaration to the contrary, such powers and duties shall be discharged by the Vice President as Acting President.

Section 4

Whenever the Vice President and a majority of either the principal officers of the executive departments or of such other body as Congress may by law provide, transmit to the President pro tempore of the Senate and the Speaker of the House of Representatives their written declaration that the President is unable to discharge the powers and duties of his office, the Vice President shall immediately assume the powers and duties of the office as Acting President.

Thereafter, when the President transmits to the President pro tempore of the Senate and the Speaker of the House of Representatives his written declaration that no inability exists, he shall resume the powers and duties of his office unless the Vice President and a majority of either the principal officers of the executive department or of such other body as Congress may by law provide, transmit within four days to the President pro tempore of the Senate and the Speaker of the House of Representatives their written declaration that the President is unable to discharge the powers and duties of his office. Thereupon Congress shall decide the issue, assembling within forty-eight hours for that purpose if not in session. If the Congress, within twenty-one days after receipt of the latter written declaration, or, if Congress is not in session, within twenty-one days after Congress is required to assemble, determines by two-thirds vote of both Houses that the President is unable to discharge the powers and duties of his office, the Vice President shall continue to discharge the same as Acting President; otherwise, the President shall resume the powers and duties of his office.

Amendment XXVI

Section 1

The right of citizens of the United States, who are eighteen years of age or older, to vote shall not be denied or abridged by the United States or by any State on account of age.

Section 2

The Congress shall have power to enforce this article by appropriate legislation.

Amendment XXVII

No law, varying the compensation for the services of the Senators and Representatives, shall take effect, until an election of Representatives shall have intervened.

APPENDIX C

list and summary of amendments

First Amendment (1791) secures the rights of freedom of speech, freedom of religion, freedom of the press, freedom of assembly, and freedom of petition

Second Amendment (1791) secures the right to bear arms

Third Amendment (1791) bans the quartering of soldiers

Fourth Amendment (1791) bans unreasonable searches and seizures

Fifth Amendment (1791) secures due process of law against federal infringement and the rules for eminent domain; secures the right not to incriminate yourself and not to be tried for the same crime twice

Sixth Amendment (1791) secures the right to a fair criminal trial, to counsel, and to confront your accuser

Seventh Amendment (1791) secures the right to trial by jury in civil cases

Eighth Amendment (1791) bans cruel and unusual punishment, excessive fines and bail

Ninth Amendment (1791) explains that just because a right is not spelled out in the Constitution, does not mean that it is not a right that a citizen of the United States is entitled to

Tenth Amendment (1791) explains that the power of the federal government is limited to what is specifically granted by the Constitution

Eleventh Amendment (1798) explains that there can be no cases brought against a state by a person who is not a resident of that state or who is a foreigner not living in the state

Twelfth Amendment (1804) explains the procedures for electing the president

Thirteenth Amendment (1865) abolishes slavery

Fourteenth Amendment (1868) explains the definition of *citizen* and establishes a punishment for government officials who became Confederates during the Civil War; secures due process of law and equal protection of the law against state infringement

Fifteenth Amendment (1870) explains that the right to vote cannot be denied based on race, color, or previous condition of servitude

Sixteenth Amendment (1913) grants the federal government the power to collect an income tax

Seventeenth Amendment (1913) provides for the direct election of senators

Eighteenth Amendment (1919) establishes Prohibition, or the ban on the manufacture, sale, or transport of alcohol

Nineteenth Amendment (1920) secures the right for women to vote

Twentieth Amendment (1933) moves the start of congressional terms to January 3 and the start of the presidential term to January 20

Twenty-First Amendment (1933) repeals the Eighteenth Amendment, ending Prohibition

Twenty-Second Amendment (1951) limits presidents to two terms

Twenty-Third Amendment (1961) provides for electors to represent the citizens of Washington, DC in presidential elections

Twenty-Fourth Amendment (1964) bans poll taxes

Twenty-Fifth Amendment (1967) explains what happens if the president or vice president is unable to perform his job

Twenty-Sixth Amendment (1971) establishes a national voting age of eighteen years old

Twenty-Seventh Amendment (1992) explains that any changes to congressional salaries will not take effect until the beginning of the next term

APPENDIX D

timeline of amendments

Timeline

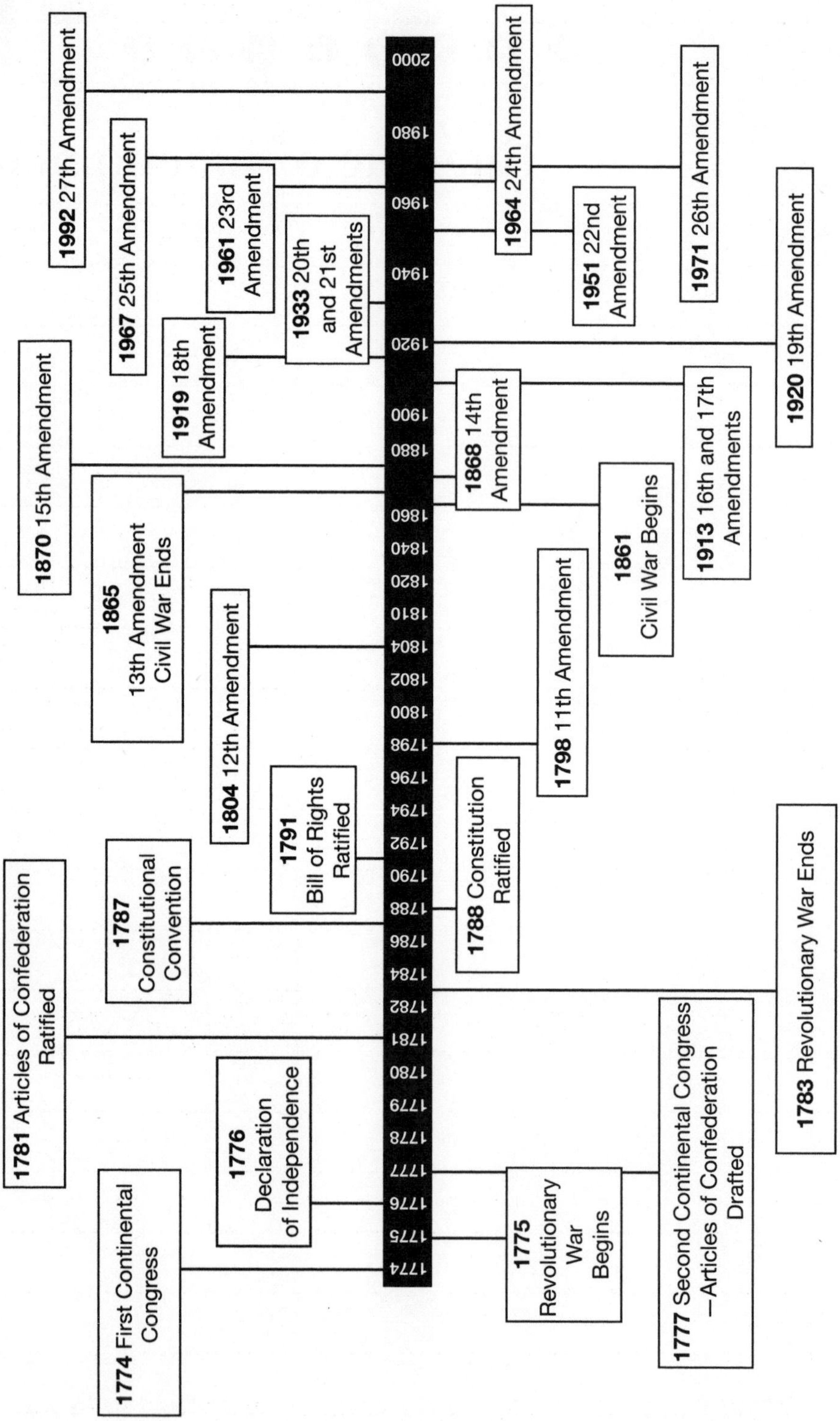
1774 First Continental Congress
1775 Revolutionary War Begins
1776 Declaration of Independence
1777 Second Continental Congress —Articles of Confederation Drafted
1781 Articles of Confederation Ratified
1783 Revolutionary War Ends
1787 Constitutional Convention
1788 Constitution Ratified
1791 Bill of Rights Ratified
1798 11th Amendment
1804 12th Amendment
1861 Civil War Begins
1865 13th Amendment Civil War Ends
1868 14th Amendment
1870 15th Amendment
1913 16th and 17th Amendments
1919 18th Amendment
1920 19th Amendment
1933 20th and 21st Amendments
1951 22nd Amendment
1961 23rd Amendment
1964 24th Amendment
1967 25th Amendment
1971 26th Amendment
1992 27th Amendment
1774
1775
1776
1777
1778
1779
1780
1781
1782
1784
1786
1788
1790
1792
1794
1796
1798
1800
1802
1804
1810
1820
1840
1860
1880
1900
1920
1940
1960
1980
2000